THE SHADOW
OF DEATH

THE SHADOW OF DEATH

Surviving Necrotizing Fasciitis

Susan J. English

⦿iUniverse®

THE SHADOW OF DEATH
Surviving Necrotizing Fasciitis

Scripture quotations marked (NIV) are taken from the HOLY
BIBLE, NEW INTERNATIONAL VERSION®. NIV®. Copyright
© 1973, 1978, 1984 by International Bible Society. Used by
permission of Zondervan Publishing House. All rights reserved.

iUniverse books may be ordered through booksellers or by contacting:

iUniverse LLC
1663 Liberty Drive
Bloomington, IN 47403
www.iuniverse.com
1-800-Authors (1-800-288-4677)

Because of the dynamic nature of the Internet, any web
addresses or links contained in this book may have changed
since publication and may no longer be valid. The views
expressed in this work are solely those of the author and do
not necessarily reflect the views of the publisher, and the
publisher hereby disclaims any responsibility for them.

Any people depicted in stock imagery provided by Thinkstock are
models, and such images are being used for illustrative purposes only.
Certain stock imagery © Thinkstock.

ISBN: 978-1-4917-3330-1 (sc)
ISBN: 978-1-4917-3329-5 (e)

Printed in the United States of America.

iUniverse rev. date: 07/28/2014

Dedication

This book is dedicated to my mother,
Nancy L. Cok,
who passed away last year after battling
advanced-stage cancer for over six years.

In her life and through her death, she taught me
about the most important things in
life: faith, hope, and love.

Thank you, Mom, for teaching me
how to love sacrificially,
how to put others before ourselves as Jesus did, and
how to have hope even in the face of adversity.

I miss you, Mom,
but look forward to seeing and celebrating
a new life with you someday in heaven.

Contents

Preface

This book is based on web journal entries that were posted to provide daily (sometimes hourly) updates to family and friends about Tom's life-threatening condition from necrotizing fasciitis, a "flesh-eating" bacterial infection. This revised edition includes additional Bible verse references, photos, and, most significantly, Tom's recollections which he journaled about a year after his illness.

As you'll read, Tom's ordeal provides strong witness to the power of prayer and the value of community. It reminds and encourages all of us to be the body of Christ, to reach out and serve others—especially those in need.

It is our hope that this book will inspire all of us to embrace and nurture our faith not only during times of crisis but every day, so that as we as grow closer to Christ, we become better equipped to travel fearlessly "through the valley," knowing God is with us always.

We extend our sincere gratitude and love to all those who held up Tom in prayer, who sent cards and notes of encouragement, and who helped in countless, practical ways as we endured this ordeal. May God richly bless each of you for your many kindnesses.

Susan & Tom English

The LORD is my shepherd; I shall not want.
He maketh me to lie down in green pastures.
He leadeth me beside the still waters;
He restoreth my soul.
He leadeth me in the paths of righteousness
*   for his name's sake.*
Yea, though I walk through the valley
*   of the shadow of death,*
I will fear no evil: for thou art with me;
Thy rod and thy staff they comfort me.
Thou preparest a table before me in the
*   presence of mine enemies:*
Thou anointest my head with oil;
My cup runneth over.
Surely goodness and mercy shall follow
*   me all the days of my life,*
and I will dwell in the house of the LORD for ever.

                                    Psalm 23 (KJV)

Summer of 1999

It was looking to be a beautiful summer, filled with lots of fun and family activities.

Our boys, ages 4, 8, and 12, had plans for camp, sailing classes, and vacation church school. I was taking graduate school classes to finish my Master's degree, and Tom had a big computer installation project at work. In late July, we had plans as a family to spend a week on a service trip volunteering and doing home repair work in the foothills of Appalachia. It looked to be a busy, but blessing-filled summer.

Little did we know in early June what "blessings" were in store for us. Little did we know that this would be the summer forever marking the *before* and *after* of our lives.

Family vacation to Florida, April 1999

June/July 1999

On June 12 and 13, Tom bicycled two hundred miles, traveling from Grand Rapids to Holland and back again the next day. This was Tom's seventh consecutive year riding in the MS 150 with some of his buddies from our church. Tom was passionate about this ride. He looked forward to this event and enjoyed raising money for the Multiple Sclerosis Society. It was a cause dear to Tom's heart since we have had both family and friends who suffered from this debilitating disease. The weather wasn't the best for the ride that weekend, but Tom finished in good time and felt great afterward.

The following weekend was Father's Day, and the boys gave Tom a nice pair of Birkenstock sandals. This turned out to be a very timely gift because, just a week or so later, Tom came down with a summer virus that caused his joints to swell and ache. All he could wear on his feet for weeks were these new Birkenstock sandals.

When the virus first started, Tom went to the doctor's office and had some blood tests done to check for rheumatoid arthritis. Thankfully the tests were negative, but the doctors did find Tom had an adult version of the virus, *fifths disease* (human parvovirus B19). The virus was nothing serious, just a common childhood illness. It had been making the rounds of the neighborhood that summer causing kids to get bright red cheeks and run a high fever. It was one of those benign summer bugs that kids pass around, but for some unknown reason Tom contracted it too. Unfortunately, there was nothing to do for it other than to rest on the couch until it passed.

A week later, still achy and sore, Tom and I made a 2-hour drive to bring our oldest son Mike to Spring Hill Camp with his cousin Dan. When we arrived, Tom had an awful time walking around the camp as his knees and ankles were so swollen and sore. We joked about him looking like an old man who needed a walker. (*We didn't know then that in a few weeks we'd actually be thrilled to see him walking at all—with or without a walker.*)

With one of our three boys gone for a week, Tom and I thought things would slow down, but every day was busy. We both had more to do than we had time or energy. My graduate classes at Aquinas College were demanding, and Tom was spending long hours at the office getting a new network installed. After work, Tom would spend the entire evening on the couch, exhausted, watching TV, while I would study and work on homework assignments. The week went by quickly, and on Friday, Mike came home from camp happy and tired.

That same weekend we hosted a going-away party at our house for Fr. Peter Vu, a young priest from our church who had been reassigned to a new parish. The turnout from our parish was fabulous—lots of people and food and fun. Tom was still limited to wearing sandals and couldn't help as much as he would have liked, but we made it through and all had a great time.

It was the beginning of the Fourth of July holiday weekend, so we headed out to the cottage the next day. Tom and I planned to spend time there with the kids for a few days and then return to Grand Rapids on Tuesday while the kids stayed at the cottage with Tom's parents.

The two older boys, Mike (12) and Steven (9), were enrolled in a sailing class at Macatawa Yacht Club for the next three weeks. Joey (4) was too young for sailing, but Grammy loved taking care of all the boys and wanted to give us a break. Tom and I planned to come out to the cottage on the weekends, but were looking forward to having our evenings free for a change. It was looking to be a really nice summer.

Two weeks went by; the boys were having a great time at sailing school and loved spending time with their grandparents. My parents had a place in Holland just down the street from Grandma and Grandpa English, so the boys had fun going back and forth between the two cottages. Unfortunately, our evenings back in Grand Rapids ended up being pretty boring. Tom didn't have the energy or ambition to do much of anything, and I had a lot of studying to do. This wasn't exactly how we'd hoped to spend our time while the boys were away with their grandparents, but that was our reality.

Still achy from the virus he'd contracted back in June, Tom woke up on Monday, July 12, complaining of a sore throat. By this time, I was tired of him being sick and wasn't ready to give him any more sympathy. Over the weekend we'd even argued about it. I complained that mothers and wives can never be sick and grumbled that even when we are really sick, we don't get to lie around feeling sorry for ourselves like our husbands do . . . I left for campus that morning telling Tom to take some ibuprofen and get over it.

Late Monday, when I returned home from campus, Tom was still feeling lousy. During the day he'd been running a fever, so he went to the doctor's office for a strep test. The strep test was negative, however, so the doctor's office just sent him home to rest.

Tuesday, July 13

On Tuesday, when I returned mid-afternoon from my classes, Tom was clearly feeling worse. His fever seemed to be gone and he looked fine, but he said his leg, just above his knee, was incredibly painful. He said it "burned" as if he'd torn a muscle. I carefully checked his leg, and although the color was a little odd, slightly grayish-pink, it otherwise looked normal. It wasn't bright red or hot to the touch. And it wasn't swollen, although with his muscular "biker" legs it was a little hard to tell. I was thinking maybe it was just a bad muscle cramp from lying around on the couch for so many days. I told him to drink more fluids, relax, and stop worrying. It was sure to feel better soon.

Later in the evening, though, Tom was still seriously complaining about the pain, so we called the doctor's service. We talked to one of the nurses, and she said that if it was a muscle pull, we should try alternating heat and ice to make it more comfortable. Through the evening we tried both, but neither the cold nor the heat seemed to be helping at all. Tom took more ibuprofen for the pain but said it was hurting *more* not less.

By midnight it was clear that there wasn't anything else to do or try, and since I had an exam the next day, I headed to bed. Tom said he'd come upstairs too and see if he could sleep, but neither of us ended up getting a good night's rest.

Here is how Tom remembers it starting . . .

After feeling lousy for weeks, I woke up one Monday morning with what seemed to be a bad cold. I was running a fever and my throat hurt whenever I swallowed. I went in to the doctor's office for a strep test, hoping an antibiotic prescription would help me get over everything, but the throat culture was negative. My temperature was over 104, and my blood pressure was slightly elevated, but I had no other symptoms, so the doctors sent me home to bed.

When I got up on Tuesday morning, I actually felt a little better. I even went into work for awhile, but by mid-afternoon, I was exhausted and decided to go back home.

As I was getting into bed, I remember doing one of those big stretches that you do in the morning. I noticed then that my leg hurt and wondered if I'd stretched too far, pulling the muscle somehow. I crawled into bed and slept for a while, but eventually went back downstairs to rest on the couch. I noticed how much my leg still hurt, but didn't think too much about it.

As the afternoon went on, I felt worse and worse. I didn't have an appetite and I couldn't rest. My leg, just above my right knee, was hurting even more than it had earlier. It didn't

9

matter what I did or what medication I tried, the pain wouldn't let up.

I decided that if it was a muscle pull, a hot bath might help, so I went upstairs and filled the tub. My leg was hurting so much by then that I had a hard time getting up the stairs. The warm bath felt good, and I soaked in the tub until the water was cold. Since my leg was still hurting, I filled the tub again, and soaked some more. When I eventually got out, I was more relaxed, but my leg wasn't any better. The bath didn't really help at all.

By this time, putting any weight on my right leg was pretty painful, so I sat on the floor to get dressed. I remember telling myself, "What a wimp. There isn't anyone here to feel sorry for you. Just get up and walk it off."

Once dressed, I tried to stand but couldn't support my weight. In the end, I scooted down the hall and down the stairs on my butt to get back to the couch. It took forever to get downstairs. When I got to the bottom of the steps, I saw a cane sticking out of our umbrella stand by the front door. It was a gag gift that someone had given to me as a joke for my 40th birthday back in February. I grabbed the cane and used it to get to the couch, thinking, "I really am old and pathetic."

5:00 p.m.

> *When Susan saw me later that afternoon, I don't think she knew what to think. She made dinner and brought mine to me in the den. I didn't have an appetite and didn't really eat much. I just stayed on the couch and tried not to move or make my leg hurt any more than it did. I couldn't concentrate enough to read or pay attention to what was on TV. We called the nurses service and were told to try applying hot/cold compresses to my leg, but it didn't help at all.*

> *A little before midnight we finally went upstairs to go to bed. We agreed that we would go to see the doctor in the morning before Susan's exam at noon. I tried to sleep, but my leg was still hurting too much. Every time I would doze off, the pain would wake me up. I finally decided to get out of bed and go back downstairs to the couch around 1 or 2 o'clock in the morning.*

> *I sat with the TV on throughout the night. I counted the hours until I could take more ibuprofen—even though it didn't seem to be doing anything to help. As the night wore on and the pain increased, I started to get nauseous. Even using the cane, I could hardly get to the bathroom in time. I was absolutely miserable.*

3:30 a.m.

> Susan came down to check on me sometime during the night. We were both puzzled by my symptoms. The pain was intense but my fever seemed to be gone. There were no marks and no swelling on my leg. Sue finally told me (again) that if it really hurt so badly, I should call the doctor . . .

6:30 a.m.

> Around 6:30 in the morning, after no sleep and no relief, I finally did call my doctor, Lee Begrow. He was a close, personal friend and I called him at his home. His wife, Karen, answered the phone and told me Lee had already left for the hospital to do rounds before his office hours began. She assured me, though, that she would relay my message to him. Within a few minutes, Lee called me back, and after a few basic questions, he offered to stop by our house on the way to his office.

7:30 a.m.

> It seemed like it took forever for Lee to get to the house. (Sue says it was less than ten minutes.) Once he arrived, Lee asked me more questions and carefully examined my leg. The pain was horrible, but he couldn't see or feel anything unusual. When he checked my blood pressure, though, Lee got a very curious look on his

face. He explained that my blood pressure was surprisingly LOW and that this could be a definite concern. He asked Sue to take me to the emergency room so they could check to see if it could be an infection, or a blood clot, or maybe just another weird virus. Lee called ahead to tell them we were on our way.

Sue packed up a few things (including books so she could study for her exam) and took me out to the garage. With her help, I made it to the van and collapsed across the back seat. A flood of emotions suddenly hit me now that a doctor had confirmed that this wasn't just in my head. I finally felt justified. It was as if this confirmation that something might actually be wrong gave me permission to admit how lousy I felt. Unfortunately this made the pain and misery feel all the more real and all the more intense.

8:00 a.m.

Blodgett Hospital is the closest hospital to our home and is the hospital where all three of our boys were born. We drove to the emergency entrance, and Sue pulled right up by the door. I hardly noticed the staff helping me into a wheelchair. The next thing I knew, I was in an examining room and they were asking questions, lots of questions.

The first nurse asked me about bug bites, and traveling, and where the pain was, and what kind of pain it was, and on and on and on. Then my vitals were taken and it was the doctors' turn to come in and ask more questions. They checked my blood pressure. Examined my leg and checked my blood pressure again. Good grief—it seemed like they kept checking my blood pressure every two minutes.

They decided they would order an ultrasound ASAP to check for a possible blood clot in my leg. While we waited, Sue tried to reassure me by saying that they would soon figure out what was wrong and would take care of it. She tried to distract me by talking about the fun we had planned for the coming weekend. We were scheduled to leave on Friday with the boys to go with friends to one of their cottages on Lake Charlevoix. We'd known these families from church for years—since our oldest boys were just toddlers—and we were looking forward to a fun, family weekend together.

Sue told me that I'd surely feel better by Friday and that I could spend the whole weekend recovering by lying on a lounge chair by the lake while the kids played in the water nearby. It sounded heavenly—a dreamy alternative to the pain that was now so intense that every muscle in my body was clenched tight in response.

After what seemed like forever, they wheeled me down the hall for the ultrasound. Sue came along, still trying to reassure and comfort me.

They began examining my leg, pushing the scanner up and down my thigh trying to see the blood vessels inside. I wanted to scream from the pain. Sue held my hand and let me squeeze hers back as hard as I needed. I vividly remember that ultrasound as it was so horribly painful. Fortunately or unfortunately, the technician couldn't find anything wrong. The scan showed nothing unusual at all. The doctor even came and looked for himself before they wheeled me back to the emergency room area.

Susan was getting worried by this time and decided to call my brother, Tim. She wanted someone from the family to know that we were at the hospital. We didn't want to worry the grandparents—as it was probably going to turn out to be nothing—but we thought someone should know where we were in case they needed to reach us about the boys.

10:00 a.m.

A new doctor, an intensivist, came in with some medical students in tow. This doctor specialized in critical care and emergency medicine and was called in to help find a diagnosis. He asked all the same questions as everyone else and then added a few new questions too. He seemed rather abrupt and not very sociable to me. He spoke more to Susan and his students than to me—which I found irritating—but I was in too much pain to complain. Before leaving, the doctor turned to me and asked if I needed anything. I told him rather curtly that "Yes—I need something for the pain." I don't even know if he responded, but he ordered more tests and an I.V. and then left the room.

The nurses drew blood and put in an I.V., and the next thing I knew they had me in a hospital gown. They told us the gown would just make it easier in case they needed to run more tests. This was getting ridiculous.

About this same time someone came in with forms for us to fill out, asking if we had living wills and advance directives. Sue and I looked at each other and wondered why in the world this was necessary right now. We'd been in the emergency room for a couple of hours by this time, and they hadn't even treated me for anything yet. The nurse said it was just standard procedure. We shrugged and set the papers aside.

Since they still hadn't figured out what was wrong, the doctors wouldn't give me anything for the pain. They told us my blood pressure was too low (and still dropping) and that they needed to find the cause of the problem before they could give me any kind of pain killers. In the meantime, my leg was killing me and we

*were getting impatient for a diagnosis. Silently,
I started to pray the rosary.*

11:00 a.m.

*The line of doctors and nurses seemed endless.
More poking and prodding—and still no pain
killers. By this time, I had a blood pressure
cuff on my arm that seemed to be taking
my pressure continuously. I was absolutely
exhausted and the pain in my leg was
excruciating. It was getting harder to stay
focused on what everyone was saying and
doing.*

*Eventually Sue slipped out to call her professor
at Aquinas to tell her she wouldn't be making it
to campus for her exam at noon.*

Noon

*At some point they moved me into a room
upstairs. My brother, Tim, had come, and he
was talking with Sue about calling my dad. I
realized then that I was not just an E.R. patient
anymore—I was now officially admitted to the
hospital. It all seemed so crazy.*

*I was thinking, what does everyone else know
that I don't know? And when are they ever going
to give me something for the pain?!? Why can't
they tell me what is wrong with my leg?!*

Sue left the room to make some more phone calls and a nurse came in. She was fussing around and I asked her what was going on. Then wham. A catheter!?! She told me it would make things "easier" for me but I didn't believe it. I couldn't believe any of this.

At some point my dad arrived. My mom stayed out at the cottage with the boys, but my parents were anxious to know what was happening, so Dad made the hour drive to come to the hospital.

Sue seemed to be going in and out of the room a lot more often now. They must have been talking to her in the hall or outside my room somewhere. I was so exhausted that I was losing track of time. I felt like I was drifting in and out. I could hardly pay attention to what was going on in the room. I was never left alone anymore. Someone was always here with me— Sue or my brother or my dad . . .

I remember someone saying they wanted to do a spinal tap. And I remember more people coming in to get me ready and asking more questions. It seemed like everyone in the room was talking at once, explaining the spinal tap procedure to me. I just kept nodding my head like I understood but I didn't. Thankfully Sue was there to pay attention because I couldn't focus on anything anymore.

If I wasn't in so much pain, I would probably have been very frightened.

5:00 p.m.

The mood had clearly become more serious. Everyone had stopped talking to me about plans for our family weekend up north. I was losing track of my surroundings and couldn't answer any more questions. Everyone seemed to know something was terribly wrong. I sensed that a lot of people were here at the hospital or were somewhere else nearby. I sensed that they wanted to help but were waiting to hear what was happening first.

Earlier in the day I was silently repeating prayers to make it through the long waiting. I was reciting Our Father and Hail Mary prayers over and over again to take my mind off the pain and to bring me strength. Now I couldn't focus to pray at all, but, strangely, I didn't feel the need to pray anymore either. Somehow I sensed that others were praying for me. I felt a sense of peace knowing that I could just surrender to the care of others, confidently trusting that everything would be okay.

I thought the doctors were talking about doing a CT scan to get a better look at my leg, but suddenly they were preparing me for surgery instead. I remember Sue giving me a quick kiss and telling me she loved me as they wheeled me out the door. I think I must have passed out on the way to surgery because that's the last thing I remember.

Wednesday, July 14
Earlier that day, shortly after noon . . .

Coming into the emergency room with Tom seemed unreal, especially since he had always been so active and was in great health overall. It was barely a month ago that he had bicycled 200 miles in just two days. He couldn't really be that sick, could he?

We waited and waited for a diagnosis so Tom could get something for the pain. The ultrasound tests had been incredibly painful. They did sonograms of his kidney's and of his entire leg from above his hip down to his ankle. I didn't know whether to hope that they would find a blood clot or to pray that they wouldn't.

During the ultrasound I tried to coach Tom to breathe like he had coached me when I was in labor for each of our three boys—but I wasn't too successful. Husbands are right about one thing—it sure is hard to see someone you love in pain.

When the E.R. nurse stayed with us during the entire ultrasound exam, continuously monitoring Tom's blood pressure, it occurred to me that either the E.R. was really slow, or they thought Tom might be seriously ill.

By late morning, Tom's brother, Tim, had come to the hospital, and by noon his dad had joined us. About that same time, the hospital staff decided to move Tom upstairs to the Intensive Care Unit (ICU). The move seemed a bit dramatic to me, but I convinced myself that it was probably because they feared Tom might have some bizarre, contagious disease. I still wasn't thinking that Tom could be in significant danger of dying. (*I was wrong.*)

When the infectious disease specialist was called in, we went through more questioning. "No, we have not eaten at any strange restaurants. No, he has no cuts or infections. No, no strange insect bites. Yes, the kids and Tom were sick a few weeks ago with a virus, but he's been feeling better, just very tired . . . No, he has no history of heart, kidney, or liver problems. No, we have not been traveling out of the country . . ." The doctors eventually decided to order more blood tests and a spinal tap to try to help make a diagnosis.

Since we couldn't see Tom for about an hour while they did the spinal tap and other tests, I decided to go over to the college to reschedule the exam I'd missed. It was only five minutes away and Tom's dad was planning to stay at the hospital. It was a beautiful summer day and I longed for some fresh air. Clearly, I didn't realize how serious things were and had no idea what was in store for us.

Halfway to the parking lot something told me not to go. As much as I'd rather be doing other things, I knew I needed to stay right at the hospital and wait this out. I turned around and walked back to the ICU.

On the way back to Tom's room, I stopped at a pay phone to call two close friends of ours, Karen and Mary, to let them know what was happening and to ask for their prayers. I still didn't realize how critical Tom was, but I did sense that it was time to get some spiritual backup support going. We needed these doctors to come up with a diagnosis and treatment plan—and we needed it NOW.

3:00 p.m.

By 3:00 that afternoon, they still didn't have a diagnosis. The spinal tap had come back normal as had the other blood tests. They were becoming increasingly concerned about Tom's blood pressure and other vital signs. They told us he was showing signs of renal and liver failure and that his blood pressure was dangerously low (90/70) in spite of the intense pain.

The ICU and infectious disease specialists were clearly frustrated, and kept looking for more pieces to the puzzle. No, we have not been traveling outside the country. No, he has not had any strange insect bites . . . But, the pieces just wouldn't fit together. Unfortunately, but understandably, the leg pain appeared to be a secondary symptom, not the cause of the problem. The Fifths Disease virus and the other symptoms he'd had recently turned out to be completely unrelated, but kept leading the doctors down the wrong path.

I remember asking at one point if there wasn't some kind of problem that would be really, really deep, in or around the bone, maybe an internal problem that wouldn't appear red or swollen on the surface. When Tom heard me, he made a wise crack about "flesh-eating disease." (*Seriously!? Evidently, he'd recently watched a TV special about necrotizing fasciitis.*) I just rolled my eyes at him, thinking that, even in such pain, he was trying to joke around.

Unfortunately, he ended up being exactly right.

5:00 p.m.

Around 5 p.m., things started happening quickly. A few of our close friends had come to the hospital to be with us. Others were near their phones waiting to hear what was going on. The doctors concluded that there might, indeed, be some kind of serious infection in his leg. If that was the case, it would explain the problems with his blood pressure, liver, and kidneys. A bacterial infection like necrotizing fasciitis produces toxins which initiate septic shock and all the major systems—liver, kidneys, circulation—start to fail. The doctors debated about taking Tom down for a CT scan to confirm the diagnosis first, but decided in the end to take him directly to surgery. I was anxious and concerned, but mostly relieved. Finally, a diagnosis.

I gave Tom a kiss and naively told him he'd be feeling better soon. I was feeling so relieved that someone was finally going to do something to stop the pain.

As they rushed Tom off to surgery, the anesthesiologist stepped back into the room to speak to me. He wanted me to realize how very serious Tom's condition was and how tenuous his vital signs were. There was no doubting this doctor—I could see the concern deep in his eyes. I was a little shocked and just stood there. As the room emptied of people, tears began streaming down my face.

7:00 p.m.

By this time, all of Tom's family and many of our friends had gathered in the ICU waiting room and hallway. It was quite a crowd.

Thankfully, the hospital staff was extremely attentive and brought me to a private room one floor above. It was a small guest bedroom room for family members where they said I could wait during Tom's surgery. They told me I could stay in this room overnight or for as long as I needed. It could be a "long ordeal," they said, and I need to "pace myself." I didn't really understand at the time what they meant. They knew what was coming—but I didn't. I had absolutely no idea how horrible the coming hours and days would be.

As I waited upstairs with my sister-in-law Mary, I remember asking her to go apologize to everyone downstairs. I felt so guilty about hiding away from all these people who came to the hospital to be with us. These were the people I know and love the most, but I just couldn't be with them. Somehow it would make the situation too real. It was too much to face. I felt supported and loved just knowing everyone was there, but I had no energy to be sociable and I didn't want to fall apart. It had been a very long day, and I was exhausted and needed to be alone. I needed to stay calm and focused.

I remember telling Mary that, for now, I was choosing to be in emotional denial about Tom's condition. It was too overwhelming to consider the alternative; too scary to accept the reality at hand. And, since the final outcome was still unknown anyway, there was no sense falling apart. I would deal with the emotional realities later. Right now, the only possible way I could help Tom would be to remain focused and clear-headed. I wanted and needed to pay attention to what the doctors said so that I could make good decisions about Tom's care. This was my mindset and was how I survived the next few hours and days.

In this midst of this turmoil, Bible verses from my childhood Sunday School classes and adult Bible studies began drifting into my consciousness . . .

> ". . . *Even though I walk through the valley of the shadow of death, I will fear no evil, for you are with me . . ." Psalm 23 (NIV)*

> "*Therefore do not worry about tomorrow, for tomorrow will worry about itself. Each day has enough trouble of its own." Matthew 6:34 (NIV)*

Lee Begrow, Tom's doctor (and our dear friend), had scrubbed up to be in surgery with Tom. About an hour into the surgery, he left the operating room and came to my room to give me an update. Lee told me that it was, in fact, necrotizing fasciitis or a "flesh-eating" bacterial infection. I thought back to Tom's comment and wondered if he had been just making a joke, or if he somehow *knew* what was wrong with him. *The Holy Spirit works in mysterious ways.*

Lee went back to the operating room and we all held our breath as we waited for Tom to make it out of surgery.

8:00 p.m.

As soon as the surgery was finished, Lee came back to my room along with Tom's surgeon, Dr. Wilcox, to deliver the official report.

"We're sorry to tell you," they said, "but the odds are against him. He has less than a 5% chance of surviving."

Evidently, Tom was so septic from the toxins this infection had been producing that all of his vital organs had shut down. He was surviving for now on life support. His kidneys, his liver, his lungs, his heart—they were all severely compromised.

The doctors told me that Tom was on a ventilator and was being closely monitored in ICU. Treatment required strong antibiotics and repeated debridement (removal) of the dead fascia tissue that was left behind from the infection. If he could make it through the next 24-48 hours, Tom would need more surgeries, but right now just keeping him alive on life support was going to be a challenge. The problem, they explained, was that this kind of infection was so aggressive and spread so quickly it was nearly impossible to get ahead of it.

It was clear that we were already behind, just starting out.

8:30 p.m.

Earlier in the evening, as soon as the doctors had narrowed down a possible diagnosis, Tom's dad left the hospital to pick up my mother-in-law from Holland. The last Dick and Irene had heard of Tom's condition was that he was on his way to surgery because of a severe infection in his leg.

I later learned that, on the way back to the hospital, Tom's parents' car broke down, and Tim had to leave the hospital to go get them. All three of them were just coming in, rushing down the hospital corridor, when the doctors met them with the news. Tom had an advanced "necrotizing fasciitis" infection in his leg . . . and he might not make it through the night.

To say they were shocked would be a serious understatement.

9:00 p.m.

Apparently, as soon as Tom went into surgery, more friends from our church were called. Word spread quickly about Tom's life-threatening condition. Within a short period of time, at least 20-30 people from our church had gathered down in the hospital chapel. Fr. Peter, the young priest for whom we'd had a going away party just a few weeks before, made the hour drive from Portland as soon as he heard the news. Prayers were offered up immediately all over town. Families, friends, adults, children—even people we didn't know—started praying.

> *"Is any one of you sick? He should call the elders of the church to pray over him and anoint him with oil in the name of the Lord. And the prayer offered in faith will make the sick person well; the Lord will raise him up." James 5:14, 15 (NIV)*

When Fr. Peter arrived, he came straight to Tom's ICU room and gave him the Anointing of the Sick, the sacrament better known as Last Rites. (*Over the coming days, Tom would be anointed multiple times by various priests. What a beautiful and powerful sacrament.*)

After he anointed Tom, Fr. Peter and I went downstairs together to the hospital chapel. There were many friends gathered there. It was a tiny chapel and was filled to capacity by that time. After we all shared a few hugs and tears, Fr. Peter led an impromptu prayer service. He began by reading a short meditation with the day's scripture reading. He told us that today, July 14, was the feast day of Blessed Kateri Tekakwitha.

I don't think any of us had ever heard of this saint before and didn't realize until later what a big part her intercessory prayers would play in the coming weeks. Father explained that Kateri was a young Native American woman from upstate New York who devoted her life to prayer and fasting. A devout Catholic Christian, she spent countless hours in the mission chapel praying for other people. On her death bed, at the young age of 24, she reassured her friends that she would continue to pray for them from heaven. Upon her death, the small pox scars that covered her body disappeared and her skin was once again pure and beautiful.

At Father's invitation we petitioned Blessed Kateri to pray in earnest for Tom's survival and his return to full health.

It was a wonderful comfort to know there were so many saints—on earth and in heaven—lifting Tom up in prayer.

10:00 p.m.

Since junior high, my favorite Bible verse has always been Philippians 4:6. Now, in the midst of this crisis, I clung to this scripture and found in these words even more profound meaning.

> *"Have no anxiety about anything, but in everything by prayer and supplication with thanksgiving let your requests be made known to God. And the peace of God, which passes all understanding, will keep your hearts and your minds in Christ Jesus." Philippians 4:6,7 (NIV)*

It seemed crazy, but, after that prayer service in the chapel, I *physically* felt the protection of the Holy Spirit over Tom and over our family. For me personally, it was as if there was a bubble or shield around me, keeping away all the anxiety and the fear. In the midst of this crisis, exhausted and worried, I felt clear-headed and focused. I felt safe. I knew in my heart that it was from the power of everyone's prayers that I was able to trust

God so completely. On my own, I would not have had it in me to be so very strong.

Returning to the ICU, I learned more about Tom's condition. I learned that during the surgery, the doctors had stripped back the thick skin over Tom's entire right thigh, leaving a large flap of flesh, in order to get at and remove the layer of decayed fascia that had been destroyed underneath. Thankfully, the infection was only in the fascia layer and had not affected the muscle or bone.

I learned that Tom's vital systems were horribly compromised and that he was on full life support. If Tom's body could withstand the assault from the toxic by-products of the infection, the doctors' plan was to go back to surgery the following day, and each day as needed, to debride more dead tissue until the infection was finally brought under control.

I started to ask the doctors how they would close the wound and how it would look later on, but the doctors dismissed these kinds of questions. They discouraged me from thinking too far ahead and told me we just need to hope *(pray)* that his body would hold out long enough to get the infection under control. For now, things were minute to minute. All we could do was pray and wait.

> *"Deliver us, Lord, from every evil, and grant us peace in our day. In your mercy keep us free from sin and protect us from all anxiety as we wait in joyful hope for the coming of our Savior, Jesus Christ." (from the Catholic rite of the Lord's Prayer)*

As it turned out, the doctors' predictions were right. Tom was barely hanging on hour to hour, and I couldn't think any further ahead than the next few minutes. It was much too scary to consider the long-term possibilities—to consider a future without Tom.

All I could do was pray . . . *This is all in your hands, God. Please help me to trust you more.*

> *"Trust in the Lord with all your heart, and lean not on your own understanding. In all your ways, acknowledge Him and He will direct your paths." Proverbs 3:5-6 (NIV)*

Thursday, July 15

1:00 a.m.

Through the night I stayed by Tom's bedside in ICU watching and waiting. His room was right across from the main desk—right in the middle of all the ICU action—but I was oblivious to everything except Tom's monitors. I quickly learned how to read each number and line: blood pressure (internal and external), oxygen saturation rate, heart rate, etc. It hardly seemed like Tom lying in that bed with all the tubes and wires and tape and bandages. Just yesterday we were home watching TV on the couch together.

I wanted to know about every piece of equipment and all his IV's, but I was careful not to ask the ICU staff too many questions. The nurses were so busy adjusting medications and ventilator settings; the last thing I wanted to do was to distract them as they cared for my husband.

I remember thinking that this was certainly not how I had planned to spend my day and my evening, but I also wouldn't have wanted to be anywhere else. It was far easier to be at Tom's side than it was to be apart from him, even if it meant just being down the hall in the waiting room. Leaving Tom's room, even for a few minutes, was unbearable. He was my "better half" and it felt like part of me was being torn away. I couldn't stand to be more than a few feet away.

"For this reason a man will leave his father and mother and be united to his wife, and they will become one flesh." Genesis 2:24 (NIV)

As the hours passed, Tom continued to hang on, but barely. His vital signs were awful—even with all the medications and assistive devices. I tried to pray on my own, but I couldn't. Where would I start? How could I begin to put my prayers into words. Thankfully, I knew that God would understand and so I just prayed . . . *Here, God, take it all—my fears, my guilt, my doubts. You sort it out, Lord. You know what I want and need. Only you know what is best for Tom and our family.*

I remembered and found great comfort in the Bible verse that says the Holy Spirit can pray for me when I can't.

> *"In the same way, the Spirit helps us in our weakness. We do not know what we ought to pray for, but the Spirit himself intercedes for us with groans that words cannot express." Romans 8:26 (NIV)*

3:00 a.m.

In the early morning hours, I finally left Tom's ICU room for a few minutes. Tom's family was taking turns staying with me in Tom's room. They had set up beds in a waiting room used for ICU families during the day, and they were trying to rest between shifts.

I was aware that Tom's family was still at the hospital but was surprised to find out that a group of close friends had stayed for an all-night vigil in another ICU waiting room just down the hall. What a consolation to find them there. I just assumed that everyone had gone home by this time. These friends had stayed and had established themselves in what had quickly become "our" waiting room.

The room was about 8 by 12 with upholstered chairs and short couches lining all the walls. Designed to offer a private space for families in crisis, the room was decorated in very subtle colors. There was just one door and no windows. Between the chairs were a few small tables with magazines and a lamp. In the center of the room was a coffee table already filled with snacks and drinks that friends had brought with them to share.

I sat down and gave everyone a brief update on Tom's condition. At this point, the medical staff was struggling to keep Tom's systolic blood pressure (SBP) above 85, but it kept dipping down to 60 or 70. They were pumping him full of fluids and giving him massive doses of "pressor" drugs (Dopamine and Norepinephrine), but his blood pressure continued to fall. They were giving Tom numerous IV antibiotics since they couldn't be sure until they received lab culture confirmation whether the necrotizing fasciitis was from Group A Strep or another type of bacteria. They had also given Tom numerous units of blood by this time and at least one unit of immunoglobulinG.

My friends could see I needed a break from all the medical statistics. And so, rising to the occasion, they filled me in on what I had been missing with them the past few hours. Here was how our friend, Karen, later described that first night in a journal entry to Tom:

When Sue called Mary and I to tell us you were in the hospital, I rushed over to Blodgett. I arrived to find you in ICU, uncomfortable with leg pain but able to talk to me. When I left at around five o'clock, they were taking you to surgery. Scott stopped by the hospital after work and then came home to pick me up. He recognized the seriousness of your condition and wanted to return to the hospital ASAP. You were in surgery when we returned. Mary and John, Brian and Betsy, Steve and Mary were all with the family when the report came that you were in critical condition with the odds against you. The news devastated all of us.

Previously a few calls were made to activate the "friends" prayer chain. Everyone helped spread the word to the rest of our IHM parish community. I contacted Fr. Julian (who was out of town), Fr. Len, and Fr. Peter. Now that the surgery report was back, Fr. Peter was called again. He came immediately to administer the Anointing of the Sick. He also led us in prayer in the hospital chapel.

As the evening wore on, many rosaries and prayers were said all over Grand Rapids for you. At the hospital, we hung on every word from the doctors and held onto every hope. The doctors were very helpful and painfully honest that you were in very, very critical condition. We were in shock—it all came on so suddenly.

None of us wanted to leave and decided we wouldn't be able to sleep anyway, so we decided to hold an all-night vigil. TJ, Steve B, Steve W, Mary, Betsy, and I stayed to laugh, cry, pray, and be with you and Sue.

Through the night we talked about the value of friendships, the power of prayer, our parish community. We made coffee runs and had deep philosophical discussions about religion and faith. We spent hours in tears, laughter, prayer, and story sharing. We prayed for you and Sue and your family too, knowing that the strength that would be needed would have to come from God.

My friends told me how by mid-evening, when people approached the receptionist at the visitor's entrance, she didn't even have to look us up in the computer to know where to send them. She would just sigh, direct them to the second floor, and announce "There are far too many people up there already!"

They told me that many people had stayed until after midnight, praying together in the chapel. I learned that TJ, Steve B., and Steve W. walked every hallway on every floor of the hospital through the night praying. Praying for Tom, our family, our friends, the doctors, the nurses, the orderlies, all the other patients and hospital staff . . . They even prayed for the custodians, refusing to stop, they said, until the whole place "dripped with the Holy Spirit."

I learned that as the night went on, my girlfriends started to reminisce about girls' sleepover nights, teasing the men and threatening to do up their hair and nails before the night was over. Evidently Steve W., when left alone with the three women, somehow became a "sister" . . . (*I never did learn what that was all about.*) Only some of my best friends could make me laugh for a few minutes in the midst of such a horrible nightmare. How blessed I felt to be supported in presence and prayer by this community of believers.

3:30 a.m.

Back in Tom's room, I struggled with what to ask for when I prayed. Was it right to ask for a miracle? Jesus said that we should. He said we should pray with complete and absolute confidence that God can do anything. But he also told us we must pray that God's will be done, not ours.

It struck me how Jesus himself struggled with this. The night before He was to be crucified, Jesus prayed fervently, asking God to remove the pending torture and humiliation. Jesus clearly pleaded with God to spare him from this torment, but, at the same time, Jesus expressed complete faith in God and obediently trusted in the divine will of the Father.

"Abba, Father," He said, "Everything is possible for you. Take this cup from me. Yet not what I will, but what you will." Mark 14:36 (NIV)

And, so, I decided to pray, asking God for a miracle with absolute confidence that God's divine judgment was better than my own. I knew that God loved our family, and if it was God's will to take Tom from us, then I would try to rest assured knowing that God has more wisdom than I have. I had to trust that He would help us make it through whatever lay ahead.

Long ago Tom and I both gave our lives to Christ. Even in the face of death—or, should I say, especially in the face of death—I found great comfort knowing that my life belonged to Him.

> *Heidelberg Catechism*
> *"Question 1: What is your only comfort in life and death?*
> *Answer: That I, with body and soul, both in life and death, am not my own, but belong unto my faithful Savior Jesus Christ . . ."*

Like Simon Peter, I was forced to admit that God was the best one to be in charge of my life. He was the one I needed to trust and to follow, even if the obstacles ahead seemed insurmountable and His plan seemed illogical.

> *"Because of this many of his disciples turned back and no longer went about with him. So Jesus asked the twelve, "Do you also wish to go*

> *away?" Simon Peter answered him, 'Lord, to whom can we go? You have the words of eternal life. We have come to believe and know that you are the Holy One of God.'" John 6:68 (NIV)*

4:00 a.m.

As the night wore on, Tom's blood pressure refused to stabilize. The ICU staff's goal was to keep his SBP above 85 or 90, but this was proving to be impossible.

Evidently, in this kind of situation, the body triggers an autoimmune response which causes the blood vessels to widen and become porous in an attempt to get rid of toxins in the blood, the by-products from the necrotizing fasciitis infection. The body wants to get these toxins out of the blood stream as quickly as possible so it dilates the blood vessels. When the blood vessels dilate, the toxins seep out into the soft tissues of the body, but they take other body fluids along. If too much fluid is lost and if the vessels dilate too much—as was the case in Tom's situation—there is not enough blood volume left in the circulatory system to maintain even minimal blood pressure. This was why the staff had to continue to pump more IV fluids into Tom while administering increasingly higher doses of blood pressure medications. The pressor drugs caused the blood vessels to constrict in an attempt to elevate the blood pressure, but for Tom it wasn't enough.

After hours of getting extra fluids pumped into him that just seeped back out again, Tom was starting to take on a puffy, bloated look, especially his face and hands. The staff was doing everything they could, but Tom's blood pressure was still dangerously low. We were fighting a losing battle.

By 4:30 in the morning, I was beyond exhausted. Everyone had been telling me I needed to pace myself and get some rest, so I finally agreed to go upstairs to the guest room and try to sleep for a while. I knew I was only one floor away, and they promised to come and get me if anything changed.

Once in the guest room, I tried to sleep. I tried to pray. I tried to cry. I was too numb and exhausted to do anything. I climbed into bed, closed my eyes, and started praying the rosary. Eventually I drifted off to sleep. I let go and let everyone else (especially our Blessed Mother Mary and Blessed Kateri Tekakwitha) do the praying for me. I gave in and let God hold all my worries for a while.

> "... and I ask Blessed Mary, ever virgin, all the angels and saints, and you, my brothers and sisters, to pray for me to the Lord, our God."
> (from the Penitential Rite)

Around 5:15 a.m., however, I was started awake by a knock on my door. *What a horrible feeling.* I had come upstairs less than an hour ago, and now my sister-in-law Mary was at the door, telling me that they wanted me back downstairs right away. She reassured me that Tom was "still here," but admitted that things were not going well. I knew that the situation must be bad if they were calling me back down to the ICU after only an hour. *Oh, dear God. Hang in there, Tom.*

When I got to his room, Tom's heart was racing. It had been pounding at over 140 beats per minute for hours, and now it was staying up at 160 beats per minute. One side effect of the high doses of blood pressure drugs was this elevated heart rate; and they had been giving him enough pressor drugs to "kill a horse" (Norepi, 58m; Dopemine, 2.5m). What was especially worrisome was that in spite of the high doses, they were still having trouble getting his blood pressure to stay above 85/60. The doctors were concerned that his heart wouldn't hold out much longer, and that his brain and other vital organs might not be getting enough oxygen. *Oh, God, help us. Help us now. Help us help him.*

I stood at the foot of Tom's bed, holding the railing for support. The nurses tried to console me as I held back tears. "It's okay to cry," they told me. No, I thought, pulling myself together again. Not yet. Not yet. He's not gone yet. I'll cry later if it comes to that . . . *Come on, God. This is it. We need a miracle. Right now would be a really good time. I know you can do it! You have the power to instantly make his body whole again. I believe that You could make him wake up and walk out of here if you wanted to, but it's up to you, God. Thy will be done. Thy will, God, but, please . . .*

> *"I tell you the truth, if anyone says to this mountain, 'Go, throw yourself into the sea,' and does not doubt in his heart but believes that what He says will happen, it will be done for*

> *him. Therefore I tell you, whatever you ask for*
> *in prayer, believe that you have received it, and*
> *it will be yours." Mark 11:23, 24 (NIV)*

The minutes passed slowly. One by one Tom's family came in to see him while our friends fervently lifted us all up in prayer. We just didn't know if Tom could make it much longer.

Quickly, a plan unfolded to get the boys to the hospital. It was important, everyone felt, for the older boys to see their dad—*now*, before it was too late. Just in case.

My parents were called. My sister-in-law, Betsi, who had spent the night with our boys in Holland, was contacted. My parents would pick up the two older boys from Betsi and come to the hospital immediately. Our younger son, Joey, the four-year-old, would stay with his cousin Lindsey and Aunt Betsi. Those three would come later in the morning, but the older boys would come with my parents—*now*.

It would take about an hour for my parents to get Mike and Steve to the hospital. Everyone prayed that Tom would hang on long enough for the boys to see him one more time.

As we waited, I thought about how I hated to have the boys see their dad like this—all these tubes, the noises, the smells and sounds and machines. Tom's face and hands were puffy from all the fluids and pressor drugs. I had lost track of how much fluid they had pumped into him to keep his blood pressure up. It was at least 10 liters so far. I hoped seeing their dad like this wouldn't be too traumatic for them. I wondered what they would think. I wondered what in the world we were going say to them when they arrived.

The clock kept ticking. And Tom kept hanging on. No dramatic miracles or flashes of light, but his heart kept pounding, and his blood pressure held, or at least stopped dropping further. I prayed that we would find the right words to say and that I would remain strong for our boys. The reality of having to bring them to the hospital to say goodbye was overwhelming for us all.

7:30 a.m.

The boys arrived sometime after 7 a.m. Lee, Tom's doctor, was with me. The hospital let us use one of the ICU staff break rooms to talk with and prepare the boys privately before we went in to see Tom. Meanwhile the nurses worked to straighten up Tom's room, hiding as many tubes and lines as they could.

Lee, "Dr. Begrow" to the boys, did most of the talking. Lee and his wife Karen had three young boys the same ages as ours. In fact, that was how we had become friends. We met years ago in the back of church when our sons were toddlers. Bringing the boys in was almost as hard for Lee as it was for me.

Lee was amazingly calm and gentle with his words. He described to the boys what they would see when they went into their dad's room—the monitors, tubes, IV's, and ventilator equipment.

He explained in simple terms what was wrong with their dad and calmly answered their questions.

When the boys were brought into Tom's room, they asked a few more questions, but were understandably very quiet. Lee again explained about the medical treatment their dad was receiving and about how all the equipment was there to help him, but was careful not to overwhelm the boys unnecessarily. He was quite candid, telling them that their dad was "very, very sick." The boys clearly understood that this was very serious. (*Later the boys told me that it was my ragged looks and puffy eyes that scared them more than anything else.*) For better or worse, they were old enough to understand.

Having the boys come to "say goodbye" was heart-wrenching for everyone—the ICU staff included. It was hard, but it went fairly well. *What a blessing to have Lee with us to help though such an awful situation.*

10:00 a.m.

The ICU staff continued to pump Tom with fluids. By mid-morning, his hands, arms, neck, and everything else had grown to at least twice the normal size. I was so thankful that the boys had come in when they did. Mike and Steve thought he looked "puffy" when they saw him, but their dad continued to grow larger in the hours that followed. The staff told me that that if Tom hung on, he'd look worse yet before he started to look better.

Researching and consulting with numerous specialists, the medical teams were creative and relentless in their attempts to keep Tom alive. Some of our family members had contacts with other research hospitals across the country. But, without fail, when someone would come up with a suggestion or a treatment, the medical staff here had already either considered or implemented it.

Tom's room was packed full of equipment and IV poles of medications. The nurses were kept busy, hustling and running their entire 12 hour shift—alarms and IV's, bedding changes and blood draws—exhausting. Despite the impossible odds, the medical staff continued doing everything possible to help Tom fight for his life.

The day continued in a blur. More tests and adjustments to medications. Meetings with doctors and specialists. Tom's parents and siblings and I all took turns sitting with Tom. It was a large ICU room, but the space was so cluttered with equipment that there was little room for more than one or two of us at a time. When the nurses weren't busy working on him, we'd pull a chair alongside the bed and hold Tom's hand and stroke his face, telling him to keep fighting.

At some point I learned that friends had stepped up the prayer chain and had scheduled a rosary prayer service for 3 p.m. that afternoon (the "Hour of Our Lord"). They were notifying as many people as possible to "storm the heavens" with more prayers.

Tom was scheduled to return to surgery around five o'clock, but, as the afternoon went on, it became clear that the infection was actively spreading. Tom was still so critical that they decided to move up his surgery time.

I gave him a kiss as they wheeled him out of the room to surgery just minutes before 3:00—the exact same time people were gathering at our church to pray for Tom. God's timing was amazing.

They later told me that church was a "full house." In the middle of a Thursday afternoon, a beautiful summer day, over a hundred people dropped everything to come and pray together for Tom. *Amazing!* Not everyone there even knew us personally, but everyone there (and those praying at home and from work) believed in the power of prayer. This was not the first trial faced by members of this community and they knew that prayer can and does make a difference.

At the prayer service, friends and strangers prayed the rosary and the Divine Mercy Chaplet. They also read, together, this beautiful petition to St. Jude:

> *Most holy Apostle, Saint Jude, friend of Jesus, we place Tom in your care at this difficult time. Pray for Tom, help him and his loved ones know that they need not face troubles alone. Please join us in asking God to send to the English Family consolation in their sorrow, courage in their fear, and healing in the midst of suffering. Ask our loving God to fill them with the grace to accept whatever lies ahead and to strengthen his faith in God's healing power. Thank you, Saint Jude, for the promise of hope you hold out to all who believe, and inspire us to share this gift of hope with others. Amen.*

Although we all wanted a miracle, I appreciated that their prayers acknowledged complete confidence and trust in God—no matter what. I was profoundly inspired by their faith and comforted by their intercessions.

3:00 p.m.

During the surgery, while everyone was gathered in prayer, I went back to my guest room upstairs to wait in private for the surgery reports.

Although I was exhausted and didn't know if I'd be able to sleep, I reminded myself that Tom—and everything else in this world—was in God's hands. Although I had no idea at the time how many people were praying, I knew our friends and families were keeping Tom and the doctors in their prayers right at this very moment.

Surprisingly, as soon as I closed my eyes, I was asleep. I slept soundly during the entire surgery, waking up on my own just minutes before the doctors came knocking on my door with their report.

I learned from the doctors that, despite his horribly unstable condition, Tom miraculously made it through this second surgery. They removed additional infected tissue down to and below his knee. Again, thankfully, the infection had only spread through the fascia layer and had not progressed into the muscle. They were unable to save any of the skin this time, but explained that skin grafts could be an option later. If he survived.

Following surgery, they started Tom on a low dose of hydrocortisone and hooked him up to a continuous dialysis machine to provide extra support for his kidneys. He was classified as "critically ill with acute renal failure and acute respiratory failure due to septic shock." It was scary to hear such a definitive label for Tom. On the other hand, it was reassuring that he had made it through the first 36 hours.

Friday, July 16

10:00 a.m.

We had been at the hospital now for over 48 hours. To keep each other informed, we started writing updates in a spiral notebook kept in "our" ICU waiting room. We used this journal to record medical updates and notes to one another so that when anyone would leave and then return, they could quickly get the latest details regarding Tom's condition.

The journal helped to eliminate the need to ask everyone to repeat the latest news over and over as people came and went from the waiting room. Tom's condition was so unstable that a lot could change just while you were away in the cafeteria grabbing some food. Having the journal helped to ensure that everyone received accurate information. Without these written journal entries we had difficulty remembering who we told which details to and what *exactly* the doctors had said. As you'd expect, the information would change slightly each time it was passed along—a frustrating version of telephone tag.

In this notebook we also recorded people's phone numbers, doctor's names, and other key pieces of information. We even designated pages in the journal for visitors to write messages to Tom since they couldn't go in to the ICU to see him.

Like me, Tom's parents and all his siblings had been at the hospital since Wednesday night. It was time that they started taking turns being here at the hospital and being away. I was "the Queen" they told me, so I could stay and could be with Tom anytime I wanted, but they would set up a schedule so family members could take shifts. This way they could provide 'round-the-clock support to Tom (and to me) without having to have everyone here all the time. It made good sense. This way they could know when to be here and when to get some sleep or take care of other responsibilities. After all, life for the rest of the world hadn't stopped in its tracks like ours had.

By this time, many people in the community had heard about Tom and were praying. At the same time, understandably, many misconceptions had arisen. I asked my family to bring my laptop computer to the hospital so I could begin posting short updates online to quell the false rumors and provide a means for people to get accurate updates on Tom. They teased me about trying to be so organized, but I teased back that it was a trait I inherited from my family. Already both families had set up schedules and systems for taking care of the kids, the cleaning, the groceries, and for taking shifts at the hospital. Impressive organizational skills—very much needed and appreciated.

Tom was scheduled to go back into surgery around 1:30 p.m. The plan was to debride (remove) any dead tissue, but it would prove to be a challenge as Tom was now HUGE. The liters and liters of IV fluid they had been pumping in to try to maintain any blood pressure, had seeped out into the soft tissues of his body making him swell-up like a balloon. Even as you watched, he seemed to grow larger.

It was hard to get your mind around how gigantic he was. It was hard to believe that the human body could expand so much, so quickly. His entire body was swollen and distended. His skin was stretched tight from all the fluid retention and it looked like he would burst if you touched him, but I did anyway. I continued to rub his hair and stroke his cheek. I knew Tom was still inside there somewhere.

It was no exaggeration to describe Tom as barely recognizable at this point. His hands were easily four to five inches thick. His head was so swollen that his ears, even as puffy as they were, could barely be seen as little indentations in the sides of his big balloon-like head. His eyes were swollen shut and his face and mouth were so engorged that a big, fat tongue stuck out between bloated lips like a cartoon drawing. The tape holding down the ventilator tube in his mouth had to be replaced every few hours because it would start pulling too much as he continued to expand in size. We had them shave off Tom's mustache as the tape had to be moved so many times that little was left of his mustache anyway. Normally weighing about 165, Tom must have weighed close to 300 lbs by this time.

Feeling guilty about making fun of Tom, but trying to process what we were seeing, our friends took to comparing him to Jabba the Hutt (Star Wars), the Stay-Puff Marshmallow Man (Ghost Busters), and Hans & Frans (Saturday Night Live). They wondered aloud and joked about whether or not he would have stretch marks once he returned to his normal size. *Sorry, Tom.*

If we had known he was going to survive, we would have taken pictures so we could show him later, but at this point it was far too morbid to consider.

4:00 p.m.

Getting Tom through surgery that afternoon was a tough challenge. Tom's lungs, like the rest of him, were not looking good. Just like everywhere else in his body, excess fluid was building up in his lungs. With so much extra fluid, even on life support with a ventilator, the staff was having a hard time getting enough oxygen into his bloodstream.

I was with Tom in his ICU room as they were preparing to take him to the operating room that afternoon. This meant that when the team switched Tom to a portable ventilator unit for the surgery and Tom crashed, I was right there to witness the whole thing.

Tom's room was typical of other ICU rooms at that time. Just inside the door was a counter with a small sink and cupboards full of hospital supplies. His bed was centered under a wall covered with plugs and tubing and outlets. On the wall opposite from his bed was a small marker board and bulletin board where the hospital staff could post messages. And, at the end of the room, in front of the windows, was a large, cushioned chair that could be used by patients transitioning from being bedridden to sitting up for short periods of time. This chair was where I would retreat when the hospital staff needed full access to Tom. From there I could see everything happening but could stay out of everyone's way.

That afternoon, as they were switching Tom from his regular ventilator machine to a smaller, portable unit for transport to surgery, all the wrong alarms went off—exactly what we had been dreading for the past two days. I watched in horror as they rushed to try to stabilize Tom, finally switching him back to the standard ventilator. Thankfully, it worked. Even though all the settings were the same, Tom's lungs couldn't handle the subtle calibration differences between the standard ventilator and the portable unit. He was that unstable.

They double-checked all the settings and, after another failed attempt and much debate, the staff decided to bring the larger ventilator machine to surgery. They would turn off all the alarms, switch Tom to the portable vent temporarily, rush his large ventilator unit down to the OR, and quickly follow behind with Tom and all his other equipment and IV poles. It was risky, but the best viable option available. We were praying that the portable ventilator would keep Tom stable enough until they could get to the OR where they would reconnect the standard ventilator.

What a circus parade it was heading down the hall to the operating room. Full-size ventilator, portable ventilator, portable BP/heart monitor, ICU bed, two IV towers with twelve pumps . . . plus half a dozen medical escorts to move everything. Thankfully, they didn't have too far to go as the ICU and OR were on the same floor in this hospital, just two hallways apart.

Witnessing this dramatic crisis was a shocking reminder to me of how incredibly unstable Tom still was and how dependent he was on these life support systems. I realized then how quickly I had become desensitized to all of the equipment in his room. That event was a serious reality check for me.

Not that I needed it, but I received another reality check just a short time later.

When Tom went to surgery, I went back upstairs to my little guest room for privacy. Once there, I realized that I'd left something in the waiting room that I wanted. My dad had Tom's cell phone with him downstairs in the waiting room, so I thought that calling it would be an easy way to reach someone. Unfortunately, my dad missed the call, and I was transferred to Tom's voice mail. "Hello. This is Tom English. I'm not available right now. Please leave a message." My heart jumped right up into my throat. I felt like all the air was sucked out of the room and I couldn't breathe. I don't remember ever feeling as horrified as I was at hearing Tom's voice. It hadn't occurred to me—not until that moment—that I might not ever hear Tom's voice again. *Oh, dear God, please help us!*

6:00 p.m.

Praise God. Tom made it through this third surgery despite his extremely unstable condition. As the anesthesiologists told me after the surgery, Tom was quite a "challenge" through the whole procedure. I think he set off a variety of alarms on multiple occasions that day.

Back in his ICU room after surgery, Tom was hooked up to even more IV pumps and devices. There were so many IV poles now that they had to bring in an extra power strip to plug them all in. Tom had also been moved to a high-tech Triadyne bed. Like the regular ICU beds, it was filled with air to help prevent bed sores. But this bed also *rocked*. Special air compartments on each side would inflate and deflate to gently move Tom from side to side, shifting the pressure of his weight from one body area to another. Although Tom had spent many hours in rough seas on his dad's sailboat, we all decided that this bed might even make Tom seasick the way it rocked back and forth.

Tom's blood pressure had stabilized around 100/60, but only because he was still on high doses of the pressor drugs (Norepi 35, Dopamine 2.5). The hospital staff explained that doses this high could cause many problems, including circulation problems to fingers and toes, so they were anxious to cut back, but Tom was still in serious septic shock and was fully dependent on the medications to maintain his blood pressure. Reducing the meds would have to wait.

The settings on the ventilator were also set very high in order to get enough oxygen into Tom's bloodstream. Fluid was collecting in his lungs, making his breathing much less efficient. The doctors, concerned about the long term effects the ventilator settings could have on his lungs, gave him a drug to induce paralysis from the neck down. This drug-induced coma would hopefully give Tom's body time to rest and recover while the machines kept him alive. We continued to pray that Tom would hang in there.

Looking back, it was hard to believe that Tom had made it through surgery that afternoon or that he had made it through the first few days at all. I sensed that God was directing the doctors and nurses somehow as they searched for solutions and worked to balance all the different medications and life support devices to keep Tom alive. Until then, I never fully appreciated how our bodies' natural systems are so delicately interdependent. As skilled and talented as this hospital staff proved to be, and as advanced as medical science is, it was clear to me that humans have only scratched the surface in understanding the wonder of God's handiwork. Our bodies are indeed beautifully and wonderfully made.

Friday, 10:00 p.m.

That evening I left the hospital for the first time since Wednesday to go home for dinner. It felt like I had been away from home for weeks.

This was the night we were supposed to meet up at Mike and MaryAnn's cottage for a weekend of family fun. Having already shopped for much of the food earlier in the week, our friends decided to bring everything over to cook up a fabulous feast for everyone here instead.

Our house was full of people helping, cleaning, and cooking. The kids were all running around with their cousins and friends. It seemed a healthy diversion from Tom's hospital room.

It was wonderful to see everyone, to get some fresh air, and enjoy a nice cold drink. But it was rather surrealistic. It was strange to have all these people at the house without Tom. Was this really happening? It almost felt like walking into a dream; at this point the hospital seemed more real to me than my own house. Or maybe I was just waking up and the hospital had been a bad dream. The emotions I felt were complex and conflicting.

I went through the house gathering things I wanted to have with me back at the hospital. On the counter in the upstairs bathroom was a daily Bible verse calendar. Still stuck on July 14, the day Tom entered the hospital, it read: *And it shall come to pass that whoever calls on the name of the LORD shall be saved. Acts 2:21 (NKJV)*

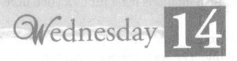

And it shall come to pass that whoever calls on the name of the LORD shall be saved.

Acts 2:21 (NKJV)

After a little while, I started to relax and unwind. I must have been home for about an hour when, in a corner of the family room, I noticed something that made me freeze. My breath caught and it felt like cold water had been thrown in my face.

The tray with the medicines, thermometer, ice pack, and drinks that Tom had used when he was first sick was still sitting on a table in a corner of the family room. With all the cleaning that people had done, no one had noticed it there, or perhaps they were unsure of where to put such personal items.

Seeing that tray made me remember what a horrible, real-life nightmare the past few days had been. The realization struck me deep, deep inside, as if a knife had been plunged into my chest. Being here wasn't a dream and neither was the fact that Tom was lying in bed back at the hospital. I quickly went upstairs, finished packing what I needed and asked Tom's brother Bill to take me back immediately.

Tom had been here, at home, just a few short days ago, and now he was in the hospital, fighting for his life. I couldn't stay home a minute longer. I needed to be back at the hospital.

Saturday, July 17

Back in the waiting room, family and friends continued to write updates to one another in the journal MaryAnn had picked up for us. Sometimes I wrote the updates, sometimes another family member would. Here are two entries, one from my brother Steve, and one from my sister Linda, who took shifts during the night staying with Tom.

Friday, 11:45 p.m. (Steve)—Progress is still slow but good. They have been pulling approximately 100 cc/hour of fluid off via dialysis and Tom's pressure is holding well. Pam (ICU nurse) is working to increase that rate while keeping an eye on his pressure. The medication used to sustain his pressure has also been reduced slightly (23 to 21). The plan is to try to reduce the amount of fluids in him (while keeping the pressure up) in order to reduce the fluid in his lungs.

Tonight I got a small scare when I was in Tom's room and proceeded to watch his blood pressure climb from mid-90's to well over 200 in a matter of two minutes. Just as I was turning to get the nurse, she returned with a doctor. Turns out this was a (natural) reaction to a dose of bicarb he'd just received. Nothing to worry about, they assured me. Sure enough, it gradually came back down over the next ten minutes.

Nothing to worry about, perhaps, but very alarming to the novice gauge-watcher.

Here is the entry my sister Linda wrote to Tom:

Tom—I thought you might want to know how the last few days have gone from my perspective. The details are already fading. On Wednesday, I learned that you were sick and in the hospital for tests. That night I heard about the surgery and a little about how very serious it was. I cried and made plans for a babysitter in the morning.

The next morning I am horrified to listen to my answering machine. A message from Steve's wife, Mary, while I was in the shower, "Linda. Page me." I page her and then listen to the message five more times to hear the recorded time of the call—waiting and worrying that the call had actually come in the middle of the night, but each time being so preoccupied with worry that I don't hear the time until the last one—7:20 a.m. Good, it has not been long. Moments later Mary calls back, "It is not good" is all that I seemed to hear or remember. I call the sitter and Frank—we are leaving now—not in one hour but NOW. They arrive at the same time and minutes later Frank and I are on our way to the hospital.

In between crying spells, I call to leave messages at work, to make kid arrangements, dog arrangements . . . Okay, my life has been notified and put on hold. I call my church to get you on the prayer chain. Done.

More worry. Why is this happening to you? Why is this happening to Sue? Why is this happening to the boys? God is preparing . . . Who? Why? Something great will come from this.

No call from Mary or Steve. Too scared to call them. I think the worst . . . He is gone and they don't want to tell me until I get there. We get to the hospital lobby and ask for directions. The clerk is concerned and informs me that there are already too many people upstairs.

Up we go to find the right area. Too many people in the hall, in the waiting room . . . I see people I know, but I barely say "hi," looking . . . looking. There is the person that I need to see—my sister, Sue. I hug her and cry the hardest cry yet. She whispers that you are still alive and I am relieved.

I settle into a chair to watch and listen. Everyone looks horrible—puffy eyes, drained, exhausted. I know that all the explanation could not explain what everyone has been going through.

I go in to see you. You look sick, but also calm and stable. Everything is going to be just fine.

The day (Thursday) continues in a hub of people, food coming in, prayer news . . . Then bad news—they think the infection has spread—must operate sooner—immediately. Numbers, stats, blood pressure, heart medicine, heart rate. Everyone up to their chins in information. Me, still on the outside looking in. Not yet understanding, not yet believing, not yet experiencing what everyone else was . . . not yet on the roller coaster.

Evening time. You are still "even"—no hiccups since surgery. A calm coming over. Not quite minute by minute anymore—Now we are going hour by hour. Everyone is exhausted and I feel like the only one still "fresh" mind, body and soul. What can I do? How can I help? Would I be able to comfort Sue? I offer, and, yes, Mary will go home tonight to sleep. I will stay. Good. Then a decision from Sue—she will stay with you until midnight, then I will stay with you until morning. Good—a job for me. Still fresh, I force myself to sleep for a few hours before midnight.

Midnight. Notebook in hand, I go to your room. Sue carefully explains each machine, each number, each detail. I scribble notes, learning and absorbing each detail. Me and you. A quiet night. I write down numbers and stats a few times an hour (in case Sue wants to know). Every person that comes in I learn what they are doing and why. I softly rub your arm. I brush back your hair. I tell you about everything going on so that you won't be worried or surprised when yet another nurse, surgeon, or respiratory therapist, takes blood or does a little tweak or turn. I grow very comfortable with your great nurse as she makes constant changes in bags, measurements, etc. I help you to be as comforted as possible. I do it as Sue would. I want Sue to know that she can sleep and you won't worry until she returns.

Your sister, Mary Jo, wakes up from an uncomfortable chair in the waiting room. We talk. You are stable. I asked for Vaseline to put on your lips—that is what I would want someone to do for me. Mary Jo goes to read and your brother, Tim, walks in. I give Tim the update—numbers, doctors, IVs . . . Everything is good. Another bell goes off. It is okay. It is just another IV on one of the three trees of eleven IV's. The nurse will change it—put on a full bag. That is how it has happened for over three hours straight. CRASH! Your numbers begin to fall. The beautiful screen of bouncing lines goes flat. The room is quiet. No alarms. No lights. I am frozen to my chair and my heart is jumping through my throat. I look at Tim—he is staring at the screen. I want him to do something— react, something. I am so glad he is there and that I am not alone. I look back to the nurse. She has the new bag hooked up. She has her fingers on the dial and she too is watching the screen. My mind is yelling. My heart is racing. I am holding my breath. Finally the silence is broken.

The nurse calmly says "Come on, Tom. Come on, Tom. Come on, Tom." The numbers start to rise. The flat lines begin to bounce again. You are stable. She says, "Well, I guess now we know for sure that Tom does not like being off that med." She started to walk out of the room like she had done one hundred times before during the past few hours. I said, "I did not like that." "Neither did I" she replied and left for more supplies.

I looked back to Tim. I said with some understanding "Is this what you have been going through? Is this more like what was happening before I got here?" Tim looked at me and said "Yes."

I was no longer on the outside looking in. I had just gotten on the roller coaster and there was no turning back.

I love you, Tom.
Linda

Saturday, 10:00 a.m.

My family kept me grounded by reporting bits and pieces of what was happening in the outside world back home and by sharing some from the kids' perspectives. Here are just a few of the tidbits they shared with me . . .

Lindsey, our six year old niece, asked her mom "Can I go to the hospital to see Uncle Tom yet?" Betsi replied, "No, Uncle Tom is still resting." Lindsey impatiently replied, "Hasn't he had enough rest already?"

My sister reports asking Steven, our nine year old, if it was strange having all those people in our house. "No," he replied, "It's just strange having the house so clean."

Our son Joey's closest friend, Charlie, reportedly told his dad, John, "I sure hope Mr. English is okay." John replied, "Yes, we hope so too." Then Charlie continued, ". . . because Mr. English always plays with Joey. His mom doesn't play at all."

Out of the mouths of babes. Evidently I worked all the time and never played with Joey, but I didn't keep a clean house either. Major humility check.

I was not about to complain, though. I felt so blessed. People were taking care of the kids, mowing the lawn, making meals for my family . . . We even had two different sets of women unknowingly come clean our house on the very same day. The bed sheets were stripped and washed again before anyone had even slept on them. I shuddered to think what people might be finding in closets and under beds, or just left scattered around the house. With my busy life, housecleaning had not been a priority. But I swallowed my pride and remained sincerely thankful for everyone's generosity and kindness. We were abundantly blessed, and I would be eternally grateful.

> *"Humble yourselves, therefore, under God's mighty hand, that He may lift you up in due time. Cast all your anxiety on him because He cares for you." I Peter 5:6, 7 (NIV)*

3:00 p.m.

Since Friday's debridement looked so clean, they just irrigated and cleaned Tom's wounds while he was in his ICU room on Saturday. No circus parade to the operating room. They looked for signs of infection, but didn't see anything new. *Hooray!*

Although the risk of pneumonia complications were still great, his lung x-rays looked "dramatically better" in the morning. They had removed a great deal of fluid and his lungs were getting more efficient. They told me his heart rate was acceptable, and the dialysis was allowing them to control and keep other blood chemicals in check.

Tom was still twice his normal size and barely fit in his fancy, rocking Triadyne bed, but he was starting to show some signs of stabilizing. His blood pressure was holding steady and they started reducing the pressor drugs (Norepi=15, Dopemine=2.5). They added a new tube that afternoon that went up his nose and down his throat into his stomach. It was a Dobbhof feeding tube to help keep Tom's digestive system active and provide some liquid nutrition until he could eat again.

We were thankful for a fairly non-eventful day.

Sunday, July 18

9:00 a.m.

Tom had a good night. The staff worked to get his blood pressure meds down even further (Norepi=8, Dopamine=2.5). And, having taken off another 2 liters of fluid through the dialysis process, some of the edema was gone and his face was starting to look more familiar. The lines across Tom's forehead were reappearing. *Hooray!*

Although the vent settings had not changed all night, the ability of Tom's lungs to absorb oxygen was improving. His O2 saturation level was coming up to within a normal range at 97. *Whew.*

And, best of all, the staff was finally talking with us about what we might expect in the days to come—something they wouldn't even consider discussing the past four days since the odds were so against Tom's survival. We were seeing some signs of hope.

1:00 p.m.

We brought in one of the boys' CD players with a huge stack of music CDs to help drown out the hum and clicks from all the machines. I alternated between playing music that was comforting to me, and playing the CDs that I know Tom liked best. Tim, one of the respiratory therapists, told me he was just glad I'm not playing too much "old people" music like they were a few rooms down the hall.

The medical staff did the irrigation and debridement in Tom's room again at noon. Since Tom had mostly returned to his normal size, the doctors and nurses could get a better look at the wound sites.

Tom's original surgeon, Dr. Wilcox, was gone on vacation, but his partner, Dr. Rodriguez, did the debridement. After the procedure, Dr. Rodriguez told me he thought Tom's calf looked a bit suspicious. He said he would have the surgical resident come back later in the afternoon to check on it and make sure everything was okay.

I immediately went in and checked Tom's lower leg myself and I thought it looked VERY suspicious. The color and skin texture looked like what I saw on Tom's leg earlier in the week. I was scared. Lee, Tom's doctor, had given me his pager number and I immediately tried to reach him, but he was at a Lake Michigan cottage with his family for the day and the signal was too weak. I called two or three times, but there was something wrong with the phone connection. They couldn't hear me and unknowingly hung up on me twice. *Oh, dear God, please help* . . .

I was starting to panic, but I was going to have to wait until later before trying to call again. My brother, Dave, had just arrived from out of town. Today was his birthday. The boys were on their way to the hospital to see me and have some birthday cake with the family. They were due to arrive at any minute. What horrible timing! I didn't want to scare the boys, so I decided not to say anything to anyone, but, as soon as I could, I would get back to the ICU and ask the nurse to call the surgical resident back ASAP. Then, I'd try paging Lee once again . . .

6:00 p.m.

Things were frantic and fearful once again. They just rushed Tom into surgery. At noon they had drawn a line around the new suspicious area on Tom's calf, and when they checked it again around 4 p.m., it had extended well past the original boundary. The infection had started just above his knee and already covered his whole upper leg. The following days it had spread across the inside/back of his right leg and now it was extending in a thin line down towards his ankle another few inches. *Will this never stop?*

In addition to the area on his calf, some black spots had developed on Tom's hands that looked like huge blood blisters. The doctors were pretty sure that the spots were just blood vessel tissue damage resulting from the high doses of pressor drugs he was given earlier, but they would take a biopsy by his left thumb while he was in surgery just to check.

Oh, pray, pray, pray . . .

9:00 p.m.

Well, one big step back. Tom made it through the surgery okay, but they did find more of the necrotizing fasciitis infection. The infection had spread down his calf and had also spread up above his hip. His groin area also showed signs of an infection although it looked less likely to be necrotizing fasciitis. They removed and will culture these tissues to confirm the diagnosis.

Having it spread down his leg, as well as farther up, past the top of his leg, was especially concerning. The doctors hadn't seriously discussed amputation—perhaps because they didn't think Tom could survive the additional trauma while in septic shock—but now that the infection has spread to his torso, even a drastic measure, like cutting off his leg to stop the spread of the infection, was no longer an option.

Right after the birthday party I was finally able to reach Lee and he had rushed back to be present during the surgery. He encouraged the surgeons to be aggressive and make sure they cut all the way to clean tissue. He even told them that we'd had our three sons, and to remove "whatever was necessary" if it looked like they needed to do so. Thankfully, that drastic measure didn't appear necessary.

The doctors didn't think these new areas were as "advanced" as the initial sites but we'd have to wait to see. They would go back into surgery tomorrow (Monday) afternoon to check more closely for any signs of continuing infection.

They warned us from the beginning to expect two steps forward and one step back, but I didn't like it. This was a very scary step backward.

Monday, July 19

Tom had a steady night. Still in a drug-induced coma, he couldn't move or respond, but seemed to be getting more stable.

He was also back in a regular ICU bed. The Triadyne bed worked great—at least for a few days. Then one compartment started leaking air. As he rotated between 20° to 25° to the left, the bed would squeal as if you were pinching a balloon and slowing releasing the air. The sound was driving all of us (including the nurses) crazy. After his surgery last night, he returned to his room on a regular ICU bed. *Thank goodness!*

Surgery was short and sweet today. The surgeon removed another small (3" square) section from his side just above the hip that looked suspicious. All of the other areas where the infected tissue was removed still looked "clean." As his vital signs remained steady during the surgery, we anticipated that during the afternoon and evening they could begin to slowly turn down the pressure and O2 settings on the ventilator. Tom was finally making progress being weaned from the blood pressure medications.

We still had no information on the biopsy they did on Tom's hand. There was definitely some skin/tissue damage from the prolonged exposure to high dose blood pressure drugs, but, thankfully, it did not appear to be necrotizing fasciitis. They continued to watch closely for any secondary infections.

As Tom began to stabilize, we started to see slight signs of hope, and the jovial nature of our friends returned. The waiting room journal now recorded a long list of people whose vacations and summer plans had been totally disrupted because of what they were calling "Tom's attention getting scheme." A group of the men were plotting to greet Tom when he eventually woke up from this coma by posting a calendar with a date ten years into the future and introducing him to some teenage boys as his sons.

Tuesday, July 20

Two steps forward. Tom was showing signs of improvement. His blood pressure (110/70) and heart rate (90) were staying within normal range. Off all blood pressure meds, Tom's heart was finally doing quite well on its own. His chest x-rays showed some improvement, so the doctors stopped the drug-induced paralysis medications. They were also starting to reduce his Ativan sedation, but warned that it would take some time for the drugs to wear off before Tom could even try breathing without a ventilator.

Tom's kidney and liver functions remained compromised, however, so the continual dialysis was still essential. A side benefit of the dialysis was that by adjusting the dialysis settings, they were able to pull off most of the extra fluids that had accumulated. Tom was looking much less bloated.

The surgeons would examine the wounds on Tom's leg later in the morning. We were praying that no new problems developed.

Sharon, one of our favorite ICU nurses, shared this verse with me:

> *"Even youths shall faint and be weary, and young men shall fall exhausted; but they who wait for the Lord shall renew their strength, they shall mount up with wings like eagles, they shall run and not be weary, they shall walk and not faint." Isaiah 40:31 (NIV)*

1:00 p.m.

After examining Tom's leg, the surgeon told us they want to move Tom from Medical ICU to the Burn Unit upstairs. The necrotizing fasciitis infection appeared to be cleared, and the medical team was concerned about getting appropriate treatment for these large, open wounds, something the Burn Unit staff was specially trained to handle.

I knew that the decision to move Tom was an indicator of stability and progress, but I was scared to leave the ICU. Everything here felt safe and had become familiar to us. We knew the doctors, the nurses, the routine . . . The ICU staff had become a life support system for all of us and I didn't feel ready to leave. The Burn Unit staff was sure to be just as caring and competent, but I didn't know them. In this unit I knew when I could come in and go out without disturbing the staff. I knew which doctors to ask which questions and I had a place for all my things in Tom's room. After all, I'd been living here for almost a week now. I knew my fears were selfish and that I needed to go along with what was best for Tom, but it was still hard. To help me move forward, I decided to go out that afternoon and get a "thank you" basket of goodies for the staff. It was one small thing I could decide and control.

I found out later that one of the key reasons for wanting to move Tom was that he had contracted pseudomonas, a "hospital bacteria" infection. The infection was at the original wound site in his right thigh and was spreading. This was a completely different kind of infection than the original necrotizing fasciitis. Pseudomonas, they told me, was aggressive and dangerous but not as destructive. In order to get the infection under control, they would need to adjust Tom's antibiotics and increase the frequency of his wound debridement (cleaning) to twice a day. Having Tom in the Burn Unit would provide the kind of expert wound care that he needed right now.

10:00 p.m.

After much discussion between all the specialists, the doctors decided not to move Tom to the Burn Unit after all. Evidently Tom was still on too many advanced life support devices and high dose meds that required ICU nursing care. The Burn Unit doctors and nurses were experts at wound care, but the ICU team members were expert at critical life support systems. As a compromise, Tom would remain in Medical ICU for now. The Burn Unit nurses would come down twice a day to do wound cleanings and dressing changes right in his ICU room. At some point, when Tom was more stable, they would move him upstairs to the Burn Unit, just not yet.

I must admit, I was selfishly relieved. I was just not ready for any more uncertainty in my life, and moving to an unfamiliar hospital floor was unsettling.

Before we heard the news, Tom's family went out and picked up a nice gift basket of goodies for the ICU staff. Even though the move to the Burn Unit had been delayed, we gave the staff the thank you basket anyway. They were surprised and very appreciative. They even told us that the next time they got hungry, maybe they would threaten to move Tom again just so they could get more treats.

Wednesday, July 21

One week. It had been one week but it seemed like a lifetime. One week ago at this time Tom had just been admitted into the hospital and was rushed off to the first of his many surgeries. Little did we know what we would have to endure in the coming days—the valley of the shadow of death.

> *The LORD is my shepherd;*
> *I shall not want.*
> *He maketh me to lie down*
> *in green pastures.*
> *He leadeth me beside the still waters;*
> *He restoreth my soul.*
> *He leadeth me in the paths of*
> *righteousness for his name's sake.*
> *Yea, though I walk through the*
> *valley of the shadow of death,*
> *I will fear no evil: for thou art with me;*
> *Thy rod and thy staff they comfort me.*
> *Thou preparest a table before me in*
> *the presence of mine enemies:*
> *Thou anointest my head with oil;*
> *My cup runneth over.*
> *Surely goodness and mercy shall*
> *follow me all the days of my life,*
> *and I will dwell in the house*
> *of the LORD forever.*
> Psalm 23 (KJV)

But, praise be to God . . . It was looking like Tom may survive. In the past 48 hours he was showing more signs of improvement. There were many dangers yet to avoid in moving through this dark valley, but we had hope.

Tom was still in a coma and very critical. His lungs and kidneys were still compromised. Most of his right leg, from ankle to above the hip, was raw flesh, an open wound that required frequent bandage changes. He had a secondary infection (pseudomonas) in his wounds. And he had developed a pressure sore on his right foot that required he wear a PRAFO/orthotic boot to keep the weight off his heel. Overall, his vital signs were slowly improving and the doctors were more confident that we had stopped the necrotizing fasciitis infection, but he was still on life support struggling to survive.

Another positive sign was that Tom was responding to pain. I wasn't there to witness it, but evidently Tom had grimaced during the dressing changes that morning— something the medical staff was pleased to see. *(That he reacted, that is; not that he felt pain.)* Up to this point Tom had been quiet and unresponsive overall. We were waiting to see if he may have even suffered brain damage from lack of oxygen. He was still under heavy sedation, but we were all anxious to see signs of him waking up. At the same time, I was nervous about what he would find when he woke up and how he might react. Those tubes down his throat were going to drive him CRAZY, and I couldn't image what his leg might feel like. The pain might be as bad or worse than when he first came into the hospital.

We prayed that he had avoided major brain damage, and that, as Tom became more and more conscious of surroundings, he would be able to deal with all the physical pain and life support devices.

Through it all, it felt like this whole ordeal must be part of God's plan. From the beginning, I knew this was bigger than just Tom and me. So many people. So many prayers. With no control or influence over what was happening, it felt like Tom and I were just along for the ride, waiting to see what would happen next. Accepting that God might be using Tom (and me) for a greater purpose made it easier somehow to cope with the crisis at hand.

Tom's Dreams & Recollections

While Tom was in his drug-induced coma, we assumed that he could not hear us and that he would have no awareness or memory of what was going on around him. As the days passed and the coma drugs were eliminated, we began to wonder about this, but still had no idea how much he was piecing together or how much he would later recall. We later learned that he was somewhat aware during parts of this time—in a fragmented, disconnected sort of way—of things that were happening around him.

> *[Tom] My last clear memory is of drifting off on my way to surgery, but I immediately think I am conscious again. I know I am very ill and Sue is taking me somewhere for help. I see us in the Chicago Airport. We just flew in and are*

waiting for something. Sue's mom and dad, for some reason, come over to us and tell us that no matter what happens, they will take care of anything we need. The next thing I know, they are gone.

I feel very weak and sad and for some reason I can't talk. Sue just holds me. We are still sitting there and Steve W. gets off a plane. He came to see us just to let us know he is praying for us. We are all very sad and Steve moves on. Sue and I continue to sit there alone.

After a while, Sue and I start walking and we end up at a train station. We meet up with our sister-in-law, Mary and her parents and my parents. We all get on the train to start some kind of journey. We are on the train for quite some time. Much of the ride is dark and underground. Sue and Mary start talking about how they have to get off the train in a few stops to go shopping for things that we will need for the rest of the journey. I'm still unable to talk or respond. I desperately do not want Sue to leave. I am afraid something will happen if she does.

The train eventually stops and Sue and Mary get off and go up the stairs. I begin to feel weaker and more helpless. We continue traveling on the train.

The train begins to have electrical problems. Lights start going out and the train is not running right. Then it happens—the train crashes. It goes right off the tracks while we are still underground. My parents and Mary's parents are fine but I can sense that I am in great danger. I am trapped. I can't move and I'm in great danger.

Mary's parents go up and leave to go find Sue and Mary. I seem to be in a predicament where if I don't get out soon I will just fade away and die. I'm not sure why, but, if not removed properly from the train I will be electrocuted. We are also in danger of another train hitting us.

I'm aware again of the train wreck . . . My father is unable to figure out a way to get me out. He says he needs to go get help before time runs out. My mom has to stay with me and make sure I don't move. I have a feeling of anxiety and feel I can't die yet, but then the anxiety becomes less and less. I realize it is not my choice but God's and if He wants me to die, I will have to obey and just go.

I hear voices. My dad is back and some emergency rescue workers are coming with equipment. It is very dark. I can see some flashlights. People are exploring the wreckage to try and figure out what to do. I'm not sure what they have planned, but it requires me to have a tube put down my throat and biting down on the end of it with all this gel in my mouth so I don't get electrocuted.

I have now totally surrendered and am ready for God's will.

There is a big flash and an electrical smell. Suddenly I am on the hood of an ambulance and a medical team is working on me. They are hooking my tube up to a ventilator. I put everything in God's hands and take the leap. But for some reason, I don't land. I haven't landed on the side of death or of life. Evidently the journey is just beginning.

Now a truck or ambulance has arrived.

My parents are no longer there. No one seems to be there with me that I know.

For some reason I think my brother-in-law Steve arranged for this truck/ambulance to get me back to a Grand Rapids hospital. I can't seem to move and it is very difficult to breathe, yet I don't panic. I am put in the back of an ambulance and there are all these people treating me saying to each other that he was in a train wreck.

I go from riding in the back of an ambulance to the back of a big pickup truck still not able to move or talk. I don't feel like I am even breathing.

Someone I know is driving the truck, a nurse maybe. She doesn't talk to me. She talks about me like someone else is there but I don't see or hear anyone else. When she looks at me she looks right through me. She looks at me as if I'm not really in my body.

We travel on. Occasionally she stops and shines a bright light in my face. I still cannot talk or move.

We continue on to some large reception. My brother Tim and his wife Liz are there. I can't move or even talk to them. They are worried that my mom will see me like this and notice that I can't move. I keep trying to tell them that it's okay and that God will take care of everything. It doesn't matter if I'm well or not.

My Mom and sister show up and don't understand why I don't get out of this truck. I want to tell them that I have to keep going on this trip.

Now I am no longer in a truck; I now am with Sue in an apartment. I am in a bed still unable to move or talk and I am in tremendous pain. Sue is talking with my sister-in-law Betsi about what doctors she needs me to see and what questions she will be asking them about my treatment. I can hear my niece, Lindsey, in the other room asking if she can come and see me. Her mother keeps telling her she can't come in yet. Sue also tells Betsi how she is going to let the two older boys come in. I try to talk but they can't hear me. It is like I am not there. They eventually say goodbye and leave the room.

I am back in the truck/ambulance again, traveling in the dark. It seems like it is always dark. I remember hearing a voice saying "you're almost there; hang in there." I see a face that I don't know with a flashlight shining on it and air being blown on my face.

The truck stops for some reason at a neighborhood on a lake and I get out. I am going from house to house looking for someone. Suddenly I am surrounded by some kind of gang. I try to run but I'm too late. While I'm fleeing, someone stabs me in the side. I'm now hiding on a porch. I move from porch to porch hiding on porches or in garages. I find that there are other people hiding there too. Everyone seems to be trying to get me away from this gang. My lower right side hurts all the way up to my ribcage. I'm bleeding and have an open wound. The people somehow get me back into the truck. We keep trying to get out of the neighborhood but the gang keeps blocking us everywhere we turn. Someone starts shouting at the gangs that my kidneys are failing and if they don't let me go I will die right there. The gang backs away and stares at me as we drive through.

Things seem to get very dark. I'm not sleeping but I don't seem awake either. I don't know where they are taking me. Are they going to take me back home or to a hospital?

The next thing I know I'm inside some type of a steel building like my warehouse at work. They have to leave me there because I am getting too large to transport in the truck. I'm having a hard time breathing.

I'm still in this building. Sue goes between holding my hand and offering encouragement and talking to people about trying to do something for me.

My mom is there squeezing my hand not saying anything. I can hear my dad in the background saying he is proud of me for hanging in there.

I must be in surgery again. No one seems to be here anymore, but I can hear a lot going on in the background. My leg really hurts and someone keeps tugging on it.

The next thing I know I am back in the back of the truck/ambulance again. It is dark and quiet. I find myself trying to say the rosary, but I can't keep track of anything. I just keep switching between "Hail Mary's" and "Our Father's." This is very comforting to me.

*I am now being taken out of the ambulance.
It is Sue getting me out. She brings me into a
small house I have never seen before. She said
someone loaned it to us while I am ill. There
seems to be music playing in the background,
some of my favorite CDs. I feel comforted, but
yet I feel like I am slipping away. I hear the
doorbell ring. It is my father. He is very sad.
He said that he just saw my Uncle Joe and my
cousin Kim, who was recently treated for breast
cancer. They have come to see me.*

*Suddenly I am back in a hospital room with
tubes all over the place, unable to move or
communicate. It's like everyone thinks my eyes
are closed and I'm unconscious. I see them come
in and try to talk to get their attention. It's like
they don't see me even though they are looking
right at me.*

*Someone always seems to be holding my hand,
but it never seems to get light out. It always
seems dark, like night. I am in constant pain, yet
there doesn't seem to be any fear. I can tell I am
never alone.*

*I am back in a dark room. I'm in a bed but I
can't move or talk. I can't tell what is real and
what is not. I have a sense that there are a lot of
people doing things for me, but I don't see them.
I know I am in constant peril, but there is this
group protecting me and helping me. It's like*

they are keeping the fear away from me so that I can take comfort in whatever will happen.

I'm back in the building again. Now I feel so big I can't breathe. I am inside the building not knowing what is going to happen to me next. I'm too big to get out of the building. Is someone going to come and get me? Will I ever get smaller? There are people here trying to get another hose down my throat. All I can think about is how I hate it when people look in my throat and how they will never get this hose in and how I will never get out of this building.

I can hear Sue in the background telling me it will be okay and that everyone is praying for me. That is the last time I remember being in that building.

I am back in a dark room. On a bed, but I can't move or talk. I hear my sister-in-law Betsi tell Sue how badly her daughter Lindsey wants to come in and see me but she is just too young. I feel something brush my feet. It is my niece— Lindsey's curly hair as she sneaks past the end of my bed. I try to tell Sue and Betsi but I can't talk and they are not looking as Lindsey sneaks in to see me.

I constantly have a sense that there are a lot of people doing things for me, but I don't see that many people. I know I am in constant peril, but I feel protected.

I am becoming aware that I am actually in a hospital room. I can hear people talking but it just sounds like background noise.

I think I can see Sue. She seems to be stroking my face and head and holding my hand. She seems to be talking but I can't hear her. I'm not sure if she can't tell that I am looking at her or if she thinks I am still asleep. It seems like other people are here but I can't see them. Maybe they are behind me.

My sister-in-law, Mary, comes in the room. Sue seems really happy to see her. They both are standing at the side of the bed smiling at me and talking but I can't hear them. It seems like the background noise is drowning them out.

The room still seems very dark. I don't seem to be able to move. I am becoming aware that there is a lot of pain.

There is still a lot of background noise, but now there is also some familiar music playing all the time. For some reason I feel very at ease—even though I'm still not sure what is really going on. I'm not sure when days end and start. I can't tell if one day or several days that seem like one have passed.

I can't seem to move at all, but I don't know if it is because of what's wrong with me or because there are so many things hooked up to me. It seems like there are tubes going in and coming out of me from just about everywhere.

Thursday, July 22

8:30 a.m.

Hooray! Tom was opening his eyes a little. He was fading in and out of consciousness and was very weak and groggy—as you'd expect—but it was exciting to see him respond.

When he first opened his eyes and looked up, I asked Tom to squeeze my hand. He barely moved his fingers. Then he tried to talk, but couldn't, of course. I explained that he was intubated on a ventilator and that they would remove it when he could breathe on his own. Rising to the perceived challenge, Tom seemed to try to take a couple of deeper breaths on his own but stopped immediately, totally exhausted.

They told us that Tom wouldn't remember any of these early days, and for that I was relieved. He was barely conscious but seemed frightfully confused and overwhelmed.

I kept reassuring Tom that we loved him and that he was getting better, not worse. That was all he needed to know for now. We didn't give him any details about what had happened or what his condition was—he was too drugged to understand any of this anyway. *What am I saying? I can't even comprehend it myself.*

From the beginning I turned my attention toward Tom's medical condition, learning about and understanding the medical issues so that I could help to make good decisions about his care. I intentionally set aside my emotional reactions to be dealt with later. Comatose for a week and unrecognizable for a while, it didn't even seem like Tom at first. I was able to successfully approach the situation from a somewhat detached, intellectual perspective—until now.

As Tom was gradually waking up, reality struck. I had been nervous about how Tom was going to react but now was suddenly overwhelmed by how quickly and unexpectedly our lives had been turned upside down. Life would never quite be the same again. But I guess that is how life is for all of us all the time, isn't it? Life is about changes and challenges and how we handle them. We would have to just take things one day at a time.

3:00 p.m.

I sat through the dressing change of Tom's wounds for the first time this morning. I had been feeling a strong need to see for myself what his wounds looked like. The medical, biology side of things didn't scare me and I felt that if I was going to help him during his recovery, I needed to fully understand what he was dealing with. So, when the Burn Unit team arrived, I just sat back in the corner in my big hospital ICU chair and didn't leave. Today's team was new to Tom's case and, since I didn't leave, they probably assumed that I always stayed in the room. They had a hard job to do and were less worried about me than Tom.

The Burn Unit team put on gowns and gloves and masks and protective eye gear and then began to remove all the bandages from Tom's leg. They slid a large plastic sheet underneath Tom as best as they could. Next, they started irrigating and spraying down his entire leg with what looked like a large water gun hooked to a two-liter saline bag. The plastic sheet caught the water and diverted it to a bucket. *I couldn't help but think to myself how our boys would love a setup like this for their water fights.*

It was unbelievable. His leg looked exactly like a muscle diagram from an anatomy book. Just like they told me, there was a large, thick skin flap pulled away from the whole upper part of his right thigh. The lower half of his leg had no skin. His shin bone was even exposed. At his hip, the open wound continued up his right side, with two or three additional areas 4-5" in diameter where the skin and tissue had been removed. Because of the fatty tissue in these areas, these wounds were deeper and looked especially gruesome. The plan was to eventually do skin grafts on his lower leg and above his hip, and to re-attach the skin flap to cover most of the wound on the top of his leg. Until all the tissue was healthy, however, they would need to continue irrigating and cleaning the raw wounds once or twice a day to keep them healthy and prepare them for the grafts.

There was some blood, but not very much. The hardest part for the team seemed to be keeping everything sterile and dry afterwards while re-bandaging his leg. There were numerous tubes and pouches and lines to work around including the ventilator, multiple IVs, a catheter, and the continuous dialysis lines. By the time they were finished, these specialists had gotten quite a workout.

As for me, I was stunned, trying to process everything I'd just witnessed. Tom's wounds had been described to me before, but now that I had actually seen them for myself, a thousand questions came to mind. How they could possibly piece Tom back together? How would they keep these open wounds from getting infected? When would he be able to walk again? How would they be able to manage his pain once Tom woke up?

It dawned on me that although Tom and I were going through this ordeal together, our experiences and our perspectives on this crisis were dramatically different. As my cousin, a thoracic surgeon from Louisville, told me when Tom was first hospitalized, I would have scars almost equal to Tom's—mine just wouldn't be visible.

I was reminded how important it was for us not to worry too much about the future. Supported by the prayers of others and the confidence that God would see us through whatever lay ahead, we had to approach the future one day at a time.

4:00 p.m.

In addition to frequent visits from the Burn Unit nurses, Tom was evidently now ready for passive physical therapy. The side effects of more than a week of complete immobility, massive drug doses, and extreme fluid retention had wreaked havoc on all of Tom's joints. His muscles were weak and useless and he couldn't have moved if he was awake and wanted to.

When the physical therapists first arrived, they moved Tom's legs for him, carefully measuring his limited range of motion. Although Tom was still heavily sedated and receiving massive amounts of pain medications, it was clear by his reactions, that the process was excruciatingly painful. *Poor Tom. When he wakes up all the way and is more coherent, he's going to think I'm absolutely crazy for being in such a good mood while he is hurting so much.*

Friday, July 23

It had been ten days since this ordeal began, and I was finally going to move out of my hospital guest room to sleep at home. Clearly this meant that Tom was doing better. I was ready to be home with the boys even though I knew it would mean lots of driving back and forth to the hospital. Thankfully, it was only a ten minute drive.

Tom was now classified as *critically stable*. The doctors believed they had beaten not only the necrotizing fasciitis (group A strep infection) but also the secondary pseudomonas infection in his leg. Unfortunately, as Tom was becoming more alert and the tissues were getting healthier, Tom's leg was becoming more painful.

I sat in on all of Tom's dressing changes now, trying to help calm him as they cleaned his raw wounds. Just like the nurses, I put on a gown and protective mask. As they irrigated and redressed Tom's leg, I would stand by his head, talk to him and hold his hand. I would play his favorite CDs and talk him through the procedure as best as I could. They were still doing dressing changes twice a day to ensure that the wounds stayed clean and healthy. Tom was heavily sedated and not really awake or coherent during these procedures. They said he wouldn't remember any of it, but I could tell it was still painful and exhausting for him. So I always stayed.

> *[Tom] One of the dreams I would have was of someone hanging me from a hook by my leg and spraying me down in the same way you might clean a freshly gutted fish. When I told*

this to Sue later, she just looked at me, paused, and finally said that this is pretty close to what they were doing each day when they cleaned my wounds.

Much later, after being home a few months, I saw an episode on TV of Law & Order where there was a burn victim in the hospital. They were preparing to do a cleaning and debridement of her wound so they put her out with anesthesia. They showed the spray gun then panned to the "Burn Unit" sign over the door while you heard water, spray, and blood-curdling screams. I immediately cringed and turned to ask Sue if that was what happened to me. I didn't think the screams could be real—after all, they had knocked the patient out. Sue had been with me, so I asked her if I screamed. Sue just looked at me for a second and quietly said "You couldn't scream. You were on a ventilator."

Saturday, July 24

10:00 p.m.

Today was a milestone day. Tom's parents came to the hospital and I left to spend the afternoon at the Dudek's cottage on Lake Michigan with the boys, my brother Steve, his wife Mary, and her sons Dan and Michael. It was my first outing with the boys in weeks.

I had very mixed feelings about the day. It was awful not seeing our boys these past two weeks, but it was so very hard to leave the hospital. Tom was getting a little stronger each day. He now opened his eyes and moved his fingers but was still disoriented and groggy most of the time. I had thought that once he was stabilized I wouldn't need to be at the hospital as much and could spend more time with the boys, but I was finding out that Tom needed me more than ever. He was fully dependent on others and was in need of comfort and reassurance.

It was a gorgeous summer day, and everyone had encouraged me to leave the hospital for a while and spend time with the boys. As Tom's pain management was still a challenge during his dressing changes, I stayed for the morning procedure. It was grueling and exhausting for everyone involved. I was relieved to think that I would miss the afternoon dressing change since I'd be with the boys at the beach.

While I was away, results from a CT scan confirmed that Tom had developed a sinus infection. The intubation tube for the ventilator had been in his mouth and down his throat for over a week and was the likely source for this new infection. As Tom still required heavy sedation and was not even close to being able to breathe without a ventilator, the doctors decided to switch to a tracheotomy tube sometime tomorrow. Hopefully, this would help clear up the sinus infection and make Tom more comfortable overall.

When I returned around 8:00 p.m., I found it had been a very busy day at the hospital and the nurses were behind schedule. Lucky me, I got to sit through Tom's dressing change after all.

I was so very, very tired on the way home that night—physically and emotionally. I didn't know if I could keep this up and I prayed fervently that God would give me the strength needed to get me through the coming days.

> *"I can do all things through Christ who strengthens me." Philippians 4:13 (NIV)*

Sunday, July 25

Tom had the tracheotomy tube inserted today as scheduled. It was a simple procedure that they were able to do right in his room. The doctors reassured us that, after a day or two, the trach would be more comfortable than the intubation tube down his throat, but at the moment it was hurting.

His kidneys were starting to produce some urine, but the doctors didn't want to take him off the continuous dialysis yet. And, the pain was still excruciating each time they changed the bandages on his leg. The medical team was trying to find an acceptable balance between discomfort and drugs, but it was a challenge.

The good news was that Tom was getting more responsive and could slowly nod or shake his head. He had been so weak that we all cheered when he was able to drag his right forearm up onto his chest earlier today. It was the most movement he'd initiated in ten days!

> *"This is the day the Lord has made; let us rejoice and be glad." Psalm 118:24 (NIV)*

As for me, I was exhausted. I found that driving back and forth to the hospital each day was especially difficult. The driving itself was fine—it was a short distance—but the transition between the hospital and home life was overwhelming.

To leave the isolated environment of the ICU and be faced with the reality of day-to-day parenting tasks in the midst of this trauma was emotionally draining. Friends and family were helping in every possible way they could—groceries, yard work, cleaning, childcare—but there were some things that only I could do as the mother. I can't imagine how much more difficult it would have been without everyone's help, but at the same time, no one could make everything all better.

One of the ways that I learned to cope with the drive back and forth was by playing Christian music CDs in the car. I cranked them up and played them really LOUD, losing myself in the lyrics. On those warm summer nights with the windows rolled down, I'll bet every house between ours and the hospital heard me drive past.

One of my very favorite songs was "Hope for the Hopeless" from a CD titled "Devotion" by the group Sierra. The four women in the group sang fabulous harmony and the lyrics were so appropriate.

Tom was hanging on and so was I. We were finding that there was hope for the hopeless.

[Tom] No, I didn't see a white light. I didn't see dead friends and family. There were no tunnels with a bright light at the end.

Was I frightened? Yes. To the point of panic? No.

In the part of my dream where I thought I would die, I remember relaxing like you do when you fall backward into someone's arms to see if they will catch you or not. I handed it all over to God. It was up to him, not me, and I knew that if I didn't have faith and give him my trust, it could be horrible. I knew God would protect me—even if it meant death.

Even before I could move on my own, the hospital staff was trying to get me moving so my joints wouldn't lock up or stiffen. I had some kind of big boot on my right foot because of a pressure sore that developed on my heel within days of my hospitalization. On my other foot I wore a huge basketball shoe to keep my leg tendons stretched. Every few hours the boot and the shoe would be taken off. When they'd been off for a while, my toes would begin to point back down and my feet, ankle, and tendons would just ache. And someone would have to put them back on me again. When they put them on, it felt just like they were breaking my feet, bending my ankle, but then it did offer some relief. They constantly moved my feet and my body to prevent additional pressure sores from developing.

Managing the pain was a constant rollercoaster. I was always being asked about my level of pain and always having meds adjusted for it, but as soon as there was some relief, it seemed like it would start to get worse again. The best was when there was enough relief that I could fall asleep for a while before the pain woke me up again. Sue was always there to record in her own journal and discuss options with the doctors and nurses. Sometimes it seemed like there just wasn't any relief. Then Sue would find some soothing music or play the rosary tape to take my mind off it all.

I remember my mouth always getting dry and sticky when I was still in ICU. I loved when people would use those little pink foam swabs to clean out my mouth.

One day I accidently sucked the water out of it. Who knew—I was thirsty and hadn't realized it. They let me try some crushed ice in my mouth and it was great. I remember how excited everyone was of that small accomplishment. I was just excited to be able to keep my mouth from drying out so much with all those tubes still everywhere.

Unfortunately I chewed up the ice too quickly just so I could get more. But it was too much of a good thing and it made my stomach feel terrible. I learned I had to leave the ice chips in my mouth to slowly melt so that my mouth would not be dry but not swallow too much so my stomach would not ache either.

It seems like a respiratory therapist came in my room every hour. When the therapist would suction off my airway through my trach, everyone would come to full alert just watching my eyes bug out of my head.

Although I couldn't move, I definitely was able to show displeasure with my eyes. I stared into Sue's eyes as I felt her squeezing my hand, telling me I was doing great and that they were almost done. The person doing the suction would apologize saying repeatedly "I'm just about done. I'm just about done." And the nurse would be saying "Oh, I know, that's just so hard . . ." My eyes definitely must have been getting the point across that this was not fun.

When they push a suction tube down your throat, you automatically have this gag reflex that seems to clamp off your throat. You feel like they are collapsing your lungs as they move the suction up and down to clean out the mucus. Once they are done they hook the vent back up, which pushes the air back in, but all you feel is air shooting out your nose and mouth but not into your lungs. I felt like I was choking and I would cough for a long time afterwards. Whenever she was in the room during these suction sessions, Sue would choose a CD to play that I like. This did help me relax and stop coughing sooner.

I remember one day when I woke up, Sue had left the room. My mom was there rubbing my hand and a nurse that I don't remember *seeing before was there with her. They asked me if I wanted something and of course I did. I tried answering and I know I was saying something but my mom and the nurse couldn't tell. I thought I was telling them I needed to get out of bed. (I still had no concept of how long I had been there and no concept that I was totally incapacitated.) I was becoming very agitated that they wouldn't help me get out of bed. My mother apologized that she couldn't understand me. I remember moving my head back and forth just trying to make people understand.*

After a while the nurse headed over and was talking in my ear telling me it was okay to be frustrated and wonder why something so bad had to happen to me and that it was normal to feel that way. I must have given her a very strange look because that thought had never crossed my mind.

I gave up trying to communicate, realizing that I couldn't get up and no one was going to get me up. Even though the nurse was wrong, it did get me to think things through a little more . . .

Gradually I was realizing how sick I was and how large my wounds were. My right leg was bandaged from my ankle all the way up past my hip to my ribs. If I wanted to move, I couldn't even adjust myself in bed without help, but anytime other people moved or jostled me, it was terribly painful.

I remember Sue trying to read my lips. With all the hoses coming out of my mouth and nose, this was impossible. I tried to mouth words, but the answers I got back didn't match what I was talking about. The nurse just kept telling me not to bite the tube.

At the time, Sue would ask a question—which I thought was at lightning speed—and I would try to mouth an answer. While I was still working on the first word, Sue would already be trying to guess what I said. As it turns out my brain was moving in slow motion. I couldn't follow them and they couldn't interpret me.

Most of the time Sue could just look in my eyes and she would know what I wanted. Sue was my voice and interpreter, my provider, and my advocate. She could tell if I needed to be moved, covered or uncovered . . . Sometimes she would sense I was trying to pray and she would turn on a rosary tape.

As I gradually stayed awake for longer periods of time, I started to pick up bits and pieces of the conversations around me. I could understand people's words, but I was confused and anxious about what I was hearing.

Everything was just so overwhelming and confusing. Still on some pretty serious drugs, I couldn't distinguish between my dreams and reality. The doctors and nurses would have very intense conversations with Sue about my care and I would wonder if there was something they weren't telling me.

Comments by people who came to visit just added to the confusion as I couldn't make sense of what they were saying. What I remembered didn't fit with what they said. It was making me increasingly anxious and nervous.

As I was becoming more alert, Sue wanted to find a way for me to communicate—especially when she was not there. Eventually my sister-in-law Mary, a speech pathologist, recommended a communication board with the alphabet on it like what she used with people who had closed-head injuries and strokes.

Sue and others would point at the letters on the board for me (as I still did not have the use of my hands) and I was supposed to tell them if it was the next letter in the word I was trying to communicate. Well, I don't think I could move my head much yet and I was still not processing everything very well. I thought they were going a million miles and hour, so I just kept trying to mouth words instead. I couldn't concentrate. Spelling out words was more than what I was ready for.

It was like a nightmare of playing charades. Everyone yelling out guesses but you couldn't move or respond to tell them if they were right or wrong. Even when they were on the right track, I had a hard time letting them know. It was all very frustrating.

Sue got me a pad of paper and a pen to see if I could write down what I wanted to say. I couldn't really feel the pen in my hand because of the nerve damage. (We didn't know yet if it would be permanent or temporary.) I couldn't hold the pad of paper while writing, so I tried to use the hospital tray table, but this was difficult to reach and was at an angle where I couldn't see it.

Sue would look at what I wrote and try to interpret my chicken scratch. She would read and repeat to me what she thought it said. Mostly she was trying to get a reaction from me for clues as she was mostly guessing. Of course, most of the time what she guessed was NOT what I wrote down. I would just keep pointing at it like she was BLIND. I thought it was clear as a bell. Of course it wasn't, but I didn't know that at the time.

I mostly communicated by moving my head side to side for "yes" and "no" and I continued trying to write out a few words. I remember one day, while Sue was away, her brother Steve kept me company. He was able to decipher my scribbles and read my lips enough to know I thought I'd been in a train wreck and that he (Steve) had arranged for the ambulance to bring me to the hospital. He did his best to explain that there wasn't any ambulance or train wreck even though I was quite insistent. Steve kept the discussion low key but made sure to tell Sue about it later.

Shortly after this incident, Sue and my sister-in-law, Liz, and a few others were visiting in my room. They started reminiscing about some of the things that happened while I was in a coma—joking about "the Staypuff-Marshmallow-Man" and other things that didn't make sense to me. Sue became very quiet and got kind of a serious look on her face. She suggested that I might be getting tired and asked everyone to slip out for a while.

Sue realized that all this talk was confusing and upsetting to me. She decided it was time to explain what had really happened.

Dreams and Telling Tom

At first, when he was coming out of the coma, we only filled Tom in on sketchy details about his condition. Then one day, when my brother Steve was with him, Tom was able to communicate that he thought he had been in a train wreck. Tom was insistent that his leg had been crushed. He knew he had been in excruciating pain and remembered it being a very frightening experience. (We found out later from the nurses that when Tom came into the ICU, they repeatedly referred to him between themselves as a "train wreck"—a common ICU phrase used to identify very critical cases.)

Tom was quite animated when he was first trying to communicate his story to us—or at least as animated as you can be when you can't talk or move and you can barely use your hands. It was obvious that this dream was very real to him. I asked Tom if I was there with him, and he told me that I had gotten off the train with my sister-in-law before it had crashed (near a shopping center, no less!). He said his mom and a few other people were there with him, but not me.

Through his scribbles Tom told us about a train, an ambulance, and a truck. He described everything as being pitch-black. He told us he could hear his mom and "the people from the train company" working to get him out.

Here are some of the scribbles telling his story:

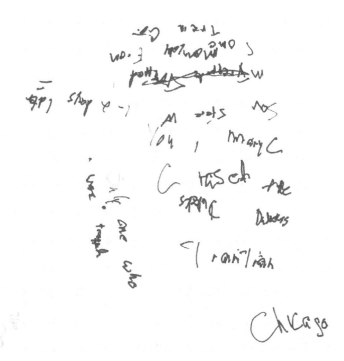

I was crushed to hear that Tom didn't think I had stayed with him. I had tears in my eyes but tried hard not to let Tom see how much his story hurt me. How awful to think that his recollections were of me abandoning him to go *shopping*, leaving him in pain and darkness, after so many hours by his bedside . . .

Soon after we realized he thought he had been in a train wreck, I told Tom what actually happened and how close we came to losing him. It was very emotional for both of us.

I might have waited longer to tell him, but visitors had been commenting on events that Tom hadn't heard about. It was confusing to him. You could see that he was trying to make sense of it, but what he heard didn't fit with his dreams.

As Tom listened to me explain what had really happened to him, tears began to stream down his face. I sat on the edge of his bed and held his hand, and we both cried. At least for a few minutes I had to face all the tragedy and the trauma we'd been through.

> *[Tom] As Sue told me the real story, I was overcome with pain and sorrow for what I had put my wife, family, and friends through these past few weeks. I had not been in a train wreck, but what had actually happened was equally scary and life-threatening. I was confused about many of the details, but was reassured that I had not imagined all the prayers and support. That part of my "dream" was true. It was of great comfort to know that my family and I had been held up in prayer by so many friends and strangers.*

Eventually I swallowed hard, gently wiped away the tears (his and mine), and tried to change the subject to talk about our future. What had happened was in the past and Tom had miraculously survived. We offered up a prayer of thanksgiving for God's many blessings to us—for the hospital staff, our friends, and our families— and asked God to give us strength and wisdom to face whatever still lay ahead.

I knew Tom would be following my lead in the coming days and weeks, so I tried to be strong. He was still critical, in intensive care, and it would be weeks before he was out of danger. I wanted to be positive and encouraging, but all I could do was cry the tears that I had been holding back these past two weeks.

In the end, Tom was the one who showed the greatest courage and faith as he wrote me one more short note:

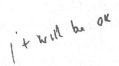

Thursday, July 29

Tom had been in the hospital for two weeks. Now that he was awake, he was keeping us all very busy. No more just sitting in the chair watching and praying and listening to CDs in a corner of his room. He wanted to communicate and was sure that his mouthing and writing was perfectly clear. Unfortunately, the scribbles were difficult to read and his spelling was awful. Tom was trying so hard to communicate, but the tracheotomy prevented him from talking, and his poor motor control prevented him from writing clearly. It was frustrating for all of us.

So far, we were not seeing any signs of brain damage from oxygen deprivation—one of our biggest concerns. Tom was recognizing everyone and seemed to understand (vaguely) what was happening around him. *Thank you, God.*

They tried taking Tom off the continuous dialysis for 24 hours, but his kidneys were still compromised and they had to restart the machine. Pneumonia remained a great risk as long as he was on the ventilator. The day before, Tom practiced breathing through his tracheotomy. They kept him connected to the ventilator for extra oxygen support, but turned off the pressure pumps so he could breathe in and out on his own.

> *[Tom] Finally after weeks on the ventilator, daily chest x-rays, and endless respiratory therapy sessions pounding on my chest and back, they've decided I'm ready to learn how to breathe on my own again. The hospital staff thinks I am strong enough now to at least try.*

> *My favorite respiratory therapist, "Kat," came in to break the news to us. Sue and Kat were excited. I was nervous. The first time would just be for a minute or two, they said, then every day they would stretch it out longer as my lungs got stronger.*

> *Kat hooked up the nebulizer-thing to the hose on my trach so I would still get moist oxygen through my trach while the ventilator was turned off. She sat me up and turned off the vent. She kept her eyes locked on mine to keep me focused and coached me on how to inhale and exhale. Sue was gripping my hand, waiting. It felt like I wasn't breathing at all. I felt panicky, but Kat said I was doing great. Calmly talking me through each breath, Kat would tell*

me it was working, even though I didn't think I was getting any air at all. She told me just to concentrate on moving my diaphragm muscles and promised to flip the vent back on if there were any problems.

Once I got a rhythm going, I found myself in a kind of trance saying the rosary in my head— the same way I had done so many times since coming to the hospital to get through something difficult. It is amazing how much reciting the rosary helped to calm my anxiety and allow me to focus on the challenge at hand.

After my breathing steadied, Kat stopped coaching quite so much and began to just let me concentrate and work on my own. She watched my stats carefully while chatting a little with Sue. I just kept concentrating like I was working to finish a marathon. Just simple breathing took all my strength and concentration.

Finally Kat turned back to me and told me I did GREAT. She hooked everything back up and turned the vent on. What a strange feeling to have the ventilator back on again—it was like someone was filling my lungs with a garden hose. Such an odd sensation. I was both relieved and exhausted.

Kat was excited. Her eyes started to tear up as she recalled how hard it was to keep me alive on the vent and all the other equipment, and now,

> here I was, breathing on my own, even if only
> for a few minutes. As would happen many more
> times in the coming weeks, I was disappointed
> by how hard it was to do something so simple,
> but everyone around me was thrilled.
>
> Sometimes this so called "progress" just makes
> me feel weaker and more helpless.

Despite Tom's progress with breathing, the hospital staff was concerned to see more fluid in his lungs. They were also concerned to see that Tom was running a fever and had developed a rash. Over the past couple of days, his whole body had gradually turned bright red, almost as if he was sunburned. They changed the PICC line and vascular catheters as those were potential secondary infection sites and sent them to the lab to be cultured.

I was still participating in most of the dressing changes, as it was complex, and managing Tom's pain was tricky. The nursing staff was amazed at what high doses of medication Tom required for pain management (150m Fentanyl patch, 25 mg Benadryl, 100 mg Seconal, plus .05 Fentanyl drip plus a 100mg bolus and 45-67 mcg IVP of Diprivan and a 150-200 Fentanyl IVP bolus to make it through the dressing change). With this much pain medication in his system, the nurses told me Tom would sleep for hours once they had finished. Surprising all of us, though, within 10-15 minutes, Tom would be awake and alert.

As Tom's white count remained low and the cultures started coming back negative, the doctors acknowledged that the rash was most likely an allergic reaction. Tom had most likely developed hives in response to one of the antibiotics or medications he was getting. They changed antibiotics (again) and waited for the rash to clear. Thankfully, as heavily medicated as Tom was, he was not uncomfortable from the hives—just bright red.

Friday, July 30

Two exciting events this day. They scheduled Tom's first re-constructive surgery for some time tomorrow, and the boys came up to visit their dad.

Tom's ICU room, by this time, looked empty to us. The dialysis machine and ventilator were still needed, but only a few of the dozen IV pumps were left in the room. From the boys' perspective, however, the room and the sight of their dad was understandably overwhelming—especially for Joey, our four-year old. It was the first time our youngest son had come into Tom's room. During the whole visit, Joey sat huddled in a chair in the corner with his grandpa.

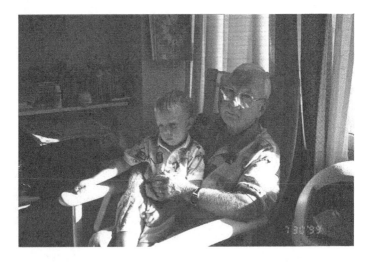

The older boys were thrilled to see their dad awake, even if he couldn't really talk or move. The last time they had seen their dad was that first early morning when they came in not knowing if he was going to live or die. The boys had been told that their dad was doing better, but now they could finally see it themselves.

Tom was still connected to a lot of tubes and could barely move his hands and arms, but it was still a great improvement. Tom could even scratch (unreadable) messages to the boys on a clipboard. The boys told Tom bits and pieces about the past few weeks, about sailing class, swimming, and sleepovers with their cousins.

For both Tom and me, the reunion brought out a surprising mix of emotions. Tom was pleased to see the boys, but it was also difficult, knowing that it was going to be a very long time before he could be fully involved in their lives again.

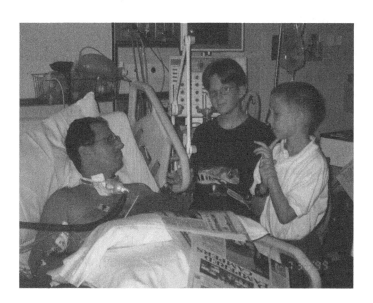

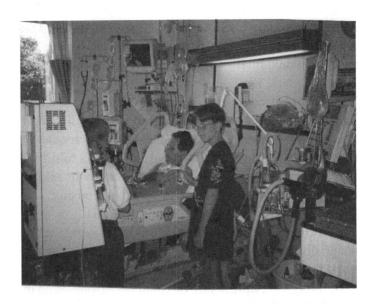

After the boys left, Tom had one of his most traumatic and painful dressing changes yet.

The medical staff told us that the longer Tom remained immobile, the more difficult it would be for him to learn to walk again. In light of this, they started physical therapy on his bad leg during the dressing change while Tom was fully sedated. Afterward, Tom had tremors all day; not just his leg, but his whole body shook for hours from the trauma.

On a positive note, Tom's hives were finally subsiding and he was no longer running a fever. Although he still had a feeding tube, they were allowing Tom to try sipping liquids (gelatin, soup, etc.). He hadn't had much more than a few tastes, but it was a start.

Skin-graft surgery would be the first step toward closing the wounds on Tom's leg. Now that he was awake and knew a little about what his body had been through, just the thought of going into surgery frightened Tom. We reassured him that he would be fine and that he had made it through numerous surgeries when he was more unstable than he was now, but, understandably, this information didn't seem to provide much comfort.

Tom's only recourse was to rally the prayer warriors. He was insistent that I ask "everyone" we knew to pray.

One couple in particular that Tom insisted that I contact was the Colligans. John and Mary Colligan, acquaintances of ours from upstate New York, were devout Catholics. They had visited our parish twice in recent years to conduct spiritual formation retreats. We had attended the retreats with many of our close friends and still talk and joke about the many things covered at those retreats (e.g. skin-to-skin nights).

The Colligans firmly believed in the power of prayer and Tom knew it. Their lives were a living example of trusting God to help them through times of terrible tragedy. One of their most recent trials was John's battle with throat cancer—a condition that was miraculously healed following much prayer and a visit to the Shrine of Blessed Kateri Tekakwitha. Tom knew the story of John's healing, but at this point, Tom hadn't been told that he had been admitted on Blessed Kateri's feast day— nor that we had been petitioning her to intercede on his behalf. *This seemed more than just coincidental to me.*

I did as Tom instructed and tracked down the Colligans, asking them to join us in prayer. They replied almost immediately via email:

> Our prayers have joined others to ask KT to intercede in your case. She was simple, humble, and a devoted follower of Jesus . . . We were at her shrine for her feast day. As you know, she worked a miracle in my life. May she do the same for you. John & Kathy

Within days we received another note in the mail along with a relic of Blessed Kateri Tekakwitha.

> Dear Sue & Tom,
>
> We are startled to learn about your affliction. We read from the website for all the information. I believe you know that Kateri had pock-marked skin all her life due to small pox at age four. As soon as she died her skin cleared up completely. She has a special intercessory role with diseases of the kind you have. We enclose her relic and urge you to touch it to the affected parts and ask her to intercede for your complete healing.
>
> We join you in those prayers.
>
> In the Father's love,
> John and Kathy

Again, what a blessing to have saints here on earth and in heaven lifting Tom up in prayer.

Saturday, July 31

Tom had his skin graft surgery around 8:30 in the morning. This was the first step toward fully closing his wounds. The surgeons were very pleased with his progress toward healing. They were able to replace the skin tissue flap on his thigh and place a skin graft to cover most of his calf by taking the skin graft from his opposite thigh. The doctors estimated that it would take 3-5 more surgeries to cover all Tom's open wounds, but they couldn't give us an exact timeline. They warned us that skin grafts often need to be redone.

Following surgery, Tom was exhausted and quiet, just sleeping off the anesthesia and extra pain medications.

Between all these surgical procedures, Tom was making good progress. He was breathing with extra oxygen but without ventilator support during the day. There were signs that they might change to a different kind of trach soon that would enable Tom to talk. He could control his hands enough to slowly scribble messages, but that was still a slow and frustrating process.

One of Tom's co-workers sent this verse:

> *"So do not fear, for I am with you; do not be dismayed, for I am your God. I will strengthen you and help you; I will uphold you with my righteous right hand."*
> *Isaiah 41:10 (NIV)*

Sunday, August 01

Overall, it was a quiet day, as Tom remained heavily sedated, but he still made some progress. The skin graft procedure went well, but Tom felt considerable pain at the donor sites. Except for the dressing change, Tom was off the ventilator all day, relying only on a trach mask with 40% oxygen. He was doing well enough that they were going to see if he could make it through the night without ventilator support as well.

Last night and this noon, he ate flavored gelatin. It tasted good to him, but I'm not sure if his stomach was ready for food. By the time I left in the evening, Tom was uncomfortable, sore, frustrated, and bloated.

As we struggled through these long days, we were comforted and inspired by so many others who've survived trying times.

We learned that Mary Quiroz, a friend of ours who was fighting breast cancer, coped during her illness by writing prayer requests from other people on index cards. She would keep them in a small box and bring them with her to her chemotherapy treatments. During her chemo infusions, she would go through the cards, one by one, saying a prayer for each person while offering up her suffering for these other people in need. *Wow.*

Tom's cousin Kim, who had multiple sclerosis and who was also recovering from chemo and radiation for breast cancer, sent Tom inspirational notes like these:

> *I think of you, Tom, when I wake up in the mornings and hear the sounds of cardinals and robins and those stupid, noisy blue jays. It won't be long before you are hearing them too, instead of the clamor of IV alarms and metal carts and things beeping and strangers' questions. The ordinary sounds of the house will never seem ordinary to you again. That is one of the things I've learned in my own dreadful experience— how to appreciate the common events in life. They really are small miracles.*

> *Recovery from near death illnesses isn't for sissies. Sometimes you get so tired of every little thing being work—but remember, every little thing is a victory. A major victory . . . ! It seemed for so long that I was making no progress at all, but now when I look back, I see that I was making advances. That's the way it's going to be with you. Every day we need to pray for patience. (I just wish patience would hurry up and get here.)*

While our day at the hospital had been long and trying, the boys had been having fun. My brother Steve had taught the two older boys how to water ski! They were so excited to tell me all about it. Tom and I were happy for the boys but sad for ourselves that we couldn't be there for the occasion and to share in all the fun. I missed my boys so much and I was tired of dealing with medical issues. *Lord, give us strength.*

> *"Cast all your cares on the Lord and He will sustain you . . ." Psalms 55:22 (NIV)*

Tuesday, August 3

Our bodies are amazing—and bizarre. Over the past day or two, the skin on Tom's hands started peeling off like snake skin. Evidently the skin had stretched so much when he retained all that fluid, that the skin layers separated and were now shedding. Pieces were coming off in large dried, chunks like a hard plastic glove that was disintegrating. Very weird, but kind of cool at the same time.

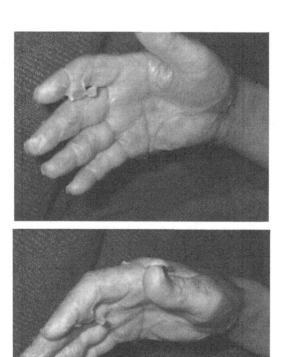

Wednesday, August 04

It had been three weeks since Tom entered the hospital. We continued to alternate between good news and bad news.

A couple of days ago they changed to a "fenestrated trach" so that Tom could talk. When he spoke, his voice sounded squeaky as if he'd been breathing helium, but it was GREAT to hear him talk. Unfortunately, the trach tube was too short and they had to replace it twice. They did this procedure in his room while he was awake . . . *Ouch.* Eventually, they had to go back to a longer trach that fit better in his throat. In God's amazing plan, before we knew Tom was going to be losing his voice again, the boys came up for another visit yesterday morning. They were able to see him and HEAR him talk. (*Joey said he sounded like Daffy Duck.*) Once again, we were in awe of God's timing and divine wisdom.

Tom had been eating small amounts of gelatin and flavored ice, but kept getting nauseous. He received all of his real nutrition through a liquid feeding tube, but the tube was no longer positioned properly. Even though it was a simple, clear-liquid diet, he was getting extremely bloated whenever he tried to eat anything. Tom felt lousy.

On top of this, Tom had developed another low-grade fever. X-rays indicated that there was fluid in his left lung, so we prayed it would not develop into full pneumonia.

Yesterday, they removed the vascular catheter and took Tom off continuous dialysis, recognizing this as another possible infection site. They had been hopeful that his kidneys would be able to function on their own, but his creatinine levels had jumped back up to 2.3 (abnormally high). It looked as if they would need to put Tom on some sort of dialysis program again, but perhaps not the same continuous CVVH system. We continued to wait and asked everyone to keep praying.

My dual life, split between hospital cares and the outside world of parenting and homeowner, was hard, but made easier by the help of so many. Everyone helped with meals, mowing, cleaning, etc. as this made it possible for me to spend time with Tom and still find moments to relax with the kids without having to worry about mundane chores. I was so very, very thankful for everyone's help. *We were so blessed.*

> *"For I was hungry and you gave me something to eat, I was thirsty and you gave me something to drink, I was a stranger and you invited me in, I needed clothes, and you clothed me, I was sick and you looked after me, I was in prison and you came to visit me . . . . The King will reply, 'I tell you the truth, whatever you did for one of the least of these brothers of mine, you did for me.'" Matthew 25:35-36, 40 (NIV)*

Dr. Wilcox, the surgeon who originally treated Tom, returned from vacation this week. He was THRILLED to see how well Tom was doing. Actually, he told us he "was thrilled just seeing that Tom was here at all." The hospital staff never expected Tom to survive that first weekend.

The doctor examined Tom and reported that his leg was ready for his second skin grafting. They scheduled it for tomorrow noon. *Hooray.*

Thursday, August 05

Tom would likely disagree, but he had a good day.

[Tom] Finally the time came for my next skin graft surgery. I was still very nervous and overall felt awful. I hadn't slept well and felt miserable. My thrashing during the night had moved my feeding tube out of position and, on top of everything else, I'd become bloated and nauseous.

Just before I was to leave for surgery, Steve Hickner, a friend of ours from church (who was also a doctor), stopped by during his rounds to visit. Sue asked him if he would pray with us before I left for surgery. Listening to Steve and Sue pray aloud, put me back into the comfort of God's hands. I again felt lifted up by others in prayer. Now I was ready.

Since I was still in ICU, they brought me directly to surgery instead of to a pre-op waiting area. The anesthesiologist unhooked my trach from the ventilator machine and connected the tube to a large "bag." Then the oddest thing happened. The anesthesiologist grinned and asked me if I'd like to pump the bag myself. I could hardly use my hands—what was he thinking?! I must have made quite a face because he quickly reassured me that he would do it and that I'd be hooked back up to a ventilator during the surgery. How odd that it felt safer to me for a machine to do my breathing than to be in control of my breathing myself.

The last thing I remembered was being wheeled into a freezing cold room and being moved onto a hard table. They put a warm blanket over me and quickly put me to sleep.

The next thing I remembered was being wheeled back down the hall to my room by two orderlies. They were laughing together and I thought that they were laughing at me. I was angry and frustrated. There were now two new tubes in my side and I hurt. I wanted to tell them to stop laughing at me. I wanted them to stop. I tried to yell at them, but of course I couldn't talk or move. I couldn't do anything.

Tom was very nervous again (understandably) about the surgery, but everything went well. They took skin from the back and side of his left leg and grafted it onto the inside and back of his right leg and calf. They inserted an NG (nasogastric) tube during surgery to help relieve some of the bloating and gas in his stomach and repositioned the Dobhoff feeding tube. (This meant Tom now had a tube in each nostril. *Yuck.*

The only areas left to close were the deeper wounds just above his hip. The doctors said it could take another 10-14 days before those areas were ready for grafting. So, we prayed that these latest skin grafts would take and that his body would soon be ready for more. The surgeon suggested we do a "skin graft dance" or whatever it was that we had been doing that had been working so well thus far. We responded, "Lots of prayers!"

The doctors said that if it wasn't for the need for more surgeries, Tom was breathing well enough on his own to remove the tracheotomy tube. But, because it had been EXTREMELY difficult to intubate Tom initially, the doctors didn't want to risk taking him to surgery without the option of using a ventilator. Thankfully, the respiratory therapist came up with a slick little valve adapter for Tom's trach that allowed him to talk once again.

Tom was hurting from all the new skin grafts and uncomfortable with the new tubes, but the bloating and nausea were gone and he was starting to heal. From my perspective at least, it was a very good day.

Friday, August 06

Tom was tired and weak all day. It was scary to see Tom getting so frail. In the big picture he was doing well, but everything took so much energy. Everyday Tom could manage more on his own—reading greeting cards and brushing his teeth—but he needed to get stronger. A two hour surgery would take its toll on a healthy person, let alone someone who's been in ICU for three weeks and who had received minimal nutrition over the preceding three days.

Thankfully, it looked like Tom's kidneys were recovering as his creatinine levels were 1.9 today. His other vital signs all remained steady and within normal ranges. We were thankful and held onto these small improvements.

During the dressing changes today, Tom got a new VAC (vacuum assisted closure) bandage on the wounds just above and below his hip. (*We have renamed him the Saran Wrap Man.*) The medical staff put a small sponge and tube into the wound and then sealed it off by covering the whole area with a clear sheet of plastic adhesive. The tube connected to a small vacuum unit. By continually extracting the air and liquids and compressing the tissues, the doctors hoped to promote quicker healing and granulation. The graft and donor sites were all looking good. Tom was (hopefully) on the mend.

Saturday, August 07

A special visitor today! Our dear friend Lydia (who used to cut hair for our family until she changed career paths to become the mother-of-quadruplets) came to the hospital and gave Tom a haircut. As he still couldn't hold his head up, Lydia could only cut the front and sides of Tom's hair. We joked that Tom might be sporting a pony tail by the time he gets out of here. But, even with a partial haircut, he looked and felt better.

Everyone's kindness and generosity was overwhelming. I knew we would never be able to remember all the kind deeds and properly thank everyone . . . I just prayed that someday, when God would present us with the opportunity to help others, we would be as eager and self-sacrificing as others had been for us.

> *[Tom] As I was too weak to move my upper body, my muscles were starting to atrophy. To stop this, the therapists made molds of both of my arms from my elbows to my hands. They had to get the plastic very warm and press it on my arms to get them shaped correctly. The warmth felt good on my skin. From the molds, they fashioned custom-fit braces with elastic bands so I could wear them when I was sleeping or resting. My arms and hands were so weak I couldn't put them on or take them off by myself but the braces were comfortable. They kept my hands more open and supported my arms.*

I was tired after all the work forming the braces and thought how nice it sounded to rest. But the therapists had other ideas. One of them took off my oversized shoe and took the brace off my bad leg. She asked me to move my foot one direction or another and ask me to point my toes up or down. None of which I could do. So, she made a note of this and then took my feet to gently move them for me. It felt like my ankle was going to break. All of the sudden this wasn't fun anymore. You would think the breaking feeling in my ankle would go away after the first time, but it didn't. She pulled and pushed my feet a few more times, taking measurements and making notes.

Then she did the unthinkable. She took hold of my bad leg to see if she could bend it at the knee. (Did she ask the doctors if she could do this?!?! Do they know what she is in here doing?!?! She can't be serious. Doesn't she know what happened to my leg and what it looks like under these bandages . . . !?) She put her hand under my knee and put a hand on my foot and began to bend it. It was one of the most painful things I had ever experienced. It actually felt like she was breaking my leg into two.

In reality, she had barely bent my knee at all.

Next, she moved over to work on my good leg— which I thought was silly—then I found out that the only way I could move even my good leg

*was with her help. I was so weak, and it was all
so very painful.*

*The last thing she did was crank my bed up so
I was almost sitting straight up. I hadn't been
upright in weeks and I couldn't believe how
uncomfortable this was. She lowered one of the
bed rails, moved all my tubes and wires out
of the way and said she was going to put my
legs over the side of the bed and turn me so I
was sitting up. Since I was mostly upright, she
worked my feet and legs slowly over to the side.
As she lowered my legs over the side, I was
unprepared for the sensation of blood rushing
into my legs and the pain from the dead weight.
My legs just hung there. I couldn't move them at
all. The pain was incredible.*

*Then she turned my torso so I wasn't leaning
against the bed, but was sitting, balancing at
the side of the bed. She and Sue were holding my
arms to keep me upright as I had no strength
at all. I couldn't believe it was true. There was
no way I could be this weak and incapacitated.
I sat balanced there at the edge of the bed,
controlled and held up by two other people.
I had no muscle control or strength at all. I
couldn't do anything on my own.*

*They held me there for only a matter of seconds,
but the pain and discomfort almost made me
pass out.*

The therapist explained that this was an initial assessment that they would use to chart out my physical and occupational therapy plan. She went on to tell me I was going to have to learn how to do everything again—not just learn to walk, but learn to sit and stand and roll over in bed. I would have to work on eating, getting dressed—anything and everything. She explained to us that because of how long I was sedated and in a coma, I had lost all my core muscle strength. On top of that, my continued immobility was causing me to lose more muscle mass and joint flexibility every day.

I couldn't believe what I was hearing. I just wanted to be home with my family and have my life back to normal again.

After the PT evaluations, they brought Tom another new contraption, a CPM (continuous passive motion) device. The CPM cradled Tom's right leg, and gently, continuously bent it for him at the knee and hip to increase his range of motion. Amazingly it was quite comfortable for Tom. He said it felt good to be moving his leg even if it wasn't under his own control.

In addition to the CPM, they made plans to increase Tom's physical therapy. As long as he remained sedentary, they told us, Tom would continue to lose muscle mass. At this point he was losing weight at the rate of a pound a day. We were told that you lose 3-5% of your strength every day that you are immobile. Tom had been flat on his back for 25 days now. Time to get moving!

Monday, August 09

It only took a week or two to learn that Mondays were busy days at the hospital. Doctors, tests, physical therapists, occupational therapists, specialists, etc. were all back in action after a weekend away. Tom woke up energetic and animated, but by the time I left for home to see the boys in the evening, he was EXHAUSTED.

Tom was making good progress, but not without some challenges. The skin grafts were taking well, but his digestive system was still giving him problems. They scheduled a barium x-ray test but decided to postpone it to another day. Instead, the doctors would try reducing his pain meds, hopeful that this might be the cause of his sluggish digestive tract.

The new CPM (continuous passive motion) device was working well. It was even quite comfortable on his leg—as long as you didn't position it too close under his backside. (*Oops.*)

> *[Tom] I remember one especially bad night. I just wanted to be home. I missed my children and would have given anything to be home with my family.*
>
> *This overwhelming depression struck me in the middle of my evening routine. It took two nurses each evening to bathe me and change my bedding. With my extensive wounds and all the tubes coming in and out of me, it was a complicated process. Just like every*

141

other evening, they rolled me to the side and draped my arm over the railing so I wouldn't feel like I was falling. This time, however, it suddenly struck me how utterly vulnerable and dependent I was. I was pressed right up against the railing with pillows helping to stabilize me. I was naked, incapable of even holding myself on my side while they washed my back. I couldn't breathe on my own. I couldn't eat. I couldn't do anything. The nurses were gentle and professional, keeping me covered as much as possible, but tonight it was more than I could handle. Humiliating and frustrating.

By this time, Sue was home with the boys, as she was most evenings now that I was more stable. My parents would come in the evenings to keep me company before I went to sleep. This night my mother was there. When she went to say goodnight, I gripped her hand and wouldn't let go. I just started to cry. She knew what was wrong right away and said "You want to be home with the boys, don't you? You miss them . . ." My mom and I cried together for some time. What I wanted most in the world was to be home holding my three boys and I felt like I was never going to get there.

I finally calmed down to where my mother could slip away. My nurse turned up the ventilator settings a little to help me sleep easier and gave me a light sedative, but I was still upset.

A different nurse who had worked with me since the beginning came in and held my hands. She looked me in the eye—her own eyes brimming with tears—and told me that she understood how set backs are hard, but that I have to remember how far I'd come. She knew my faith was strong and would pull me through. She reminded me how many people were praying for me still and reassured me that I would make it home to my boys someday. We cried some more and I finally started to relax.

I realized then that I hadn't been relying on my faith enough. I was just feeling sorry for myself, and that is what had made the day and my life ahead look so bleak. I needed to trust God and put my faith in him—every minute, every day. I thank God that He sent people like this caring nurse to remind me.

Tuesday, August 10

Rats—another step back.

During the night, Tom started running a low grade fever and was quite fitful. He was restless enough to grab the NG and feeding tubes in his nose and pull them out of position. He pulled them out just far enough that they had to remove both tubes. They tried to replace the feeding tube, but it wasn't positioned correctly. Tom tried to eat a little on his own, but it was making him nauseous.

Tomorrow they would reevaluate Tom's digestion/feeding issues. In order to fuel the healing process, it was essential for Tom to get adequate nutrition, so the situation was both frustrating and urgent.

Despite the setback, the doctors were confident that Tom was on his way to a full recovery. We just wanted it to happen FASTER. Through it all, we continued to find great comfort in knowing God was in control. We reminded ourselves that His timing is not always our timing. We prayed for patience.

> *"There is a time for everything, and a season for every activity under heaven." Ecclesiastes 3:1 (NIV)*

Wednesday, August 11

I woke up in the middle of the night and prayed and pleaded that God would bring Tom home soon. I was feeling so very tired of all of this.

Four weeks ago, Tom was admitted to the hospital. He had been improving over the past few weeks, but it was so exhausting. Every day I woke up early so I could get to the hospital first thing in the morning to catch the nursing staff. All day and through the evening I would feel torn about whether to stay or go home to be with the boys. On top of that, Tom was feeling lousy—physically and emotionally. I just didn't know how much longer we could keep this up.

On the way to the hospital, I again blasted my new, favorite CD, "Devotion" by Sierra. I found hope and inspiration in the lyrics from the song "You Know What I Need" . . . and God did hear me. He did know.

When I arrived at the hospital I learned that Tom had gotten a great pep talk last night from a close friend, and again this morning from his doctor (our good friend, Lee). Afterwards, Tom really hung tough through the dressing change on his leg, and he seemed inspired to work even harder to get better.

Around 11 a.m., the surgeon stopped by and told us that not only was Tom doing fine, but that he may not need any more surgeries. (*Hooray Hooray*) He said if the remaining wounds don't close on their own, they could probably graft the sites under local anesthesia.

Within five minutes the ICU team came in and removed Tom's tracheotomy. We all cried tears of joy. *HALLELUIAH*

Tom was now down to just one IV drip and a feeding tube. (At one point, remember, he had 12 different IV pumps plus multiple life support devices.) An ultrasound test on his liver and gallbladder looked normal. Recent lab cultures showed no signs of staph or strep infections. His creatinine levels were now within the high-normal range without dialysis support. And his stomach was (hopefully) settling down.

In the afternoon, the physical and occupational therapists started Tom on a rigorous rehabilitation program—bending both legs, doing arm exercises, and sitting up at the side of the bed—for 12 minutes! Tom's muscles and joints were screaming with the pain, and he was exhausted, but it was a welcome relief to be entering a new recovery phase at last.

> *"I am the Lord, the God of all mankind, is anything too hard for me?"*
> Jeremiah 32:27 (NIV)

It would be a long, HARD road ahead to recovery, but Tom and I both knew that God had been and would continue to be with us every step of the way. God had a plan for us, and we knew that however hard it might be, He knew just what we needed. Just like children with a parent, we needed to trust Him. As our loving Father He would lead us where we needed to go and would provide us with all that we required.

Thursday, August 12

It was another good day. Tom was so exhausted he fell asleep eating his dinner (jello), but that was a good sign this time.

Simple things, like lifting and turning his head when the nurses changed pillows, or brushing his teeth, or shifting in bed were still difficult. All the little activities added up and wore him out physically. Very slowly he was doing more on his own.

As they continued to reduce his pain medications, Tom's dressing changes became more grueling. Each time they redressed the vacuum closure on his hip, they had to rip off the large plastic adhesive sheet that allowed the vacuum to work. Each time they tore it off, it removed more of the hair along his side and stomach. *Ouch.*

The best part of Tom's day—without a doubt—was when the boys came up to visit in the afternoon. They were thrilled to see their dad without a trach and with fewer machines in the room. The older boys chatted with Tom while little Joey cuddled next to his dad in bed and watched cartoons. The boys told me later that "he seemed more like Dad." What a wonderful sight for me to see all my boys together for a few minutes.

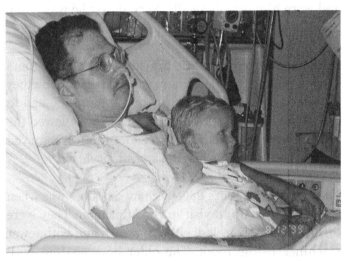

Friday, August 13

Tom was scheduled to be moved to the burn unit within the next few days as he was no longer in "critical condition." He did not need ventilator or oxygen support, dialysis, blood pressure med's, or IV pain med's, and he was almost ready to do without the feeding tube. *Hooray!*

Tom's creatinine level was back to normal (1.0). During those first few weeks, the nephrologist (kidney specialist) told us that he expected that Tom's kidneys would eventually be fully functional, but that it could easily take months to recover from this kind of septic shock trauma. *Sola deo gloria.*

And he finally made his 1,000 calorie intake goal. His stomach and digestive system were still sluggish and he was often nauseous, but the hospital staff was not surprised given the high levels of pain medication he required. Tom was in no hurry to have the Dobbhoff feeding tube removed, however, as he did NOT want that thing shoved up his nose ever again.

With the exception of all the special supplies for his bandages and his rehab equipment, his ICU room was quite empty now. He did have a PICC line for IV's, a Foley catheter, a heart/O2 monitor, and was still connected with tubes to the VAC pump, but it was a far different picture than just a few weeks ago.

Tom had a good physical therapy workout today—sitting on the edge of the bed for 17 minutes and standing (with assistance) for 13 seconds. Not bad after 30 straight days in bed. A number of things would be reevaluated on Monday: moving to another unit, antibiotics, rehab plan, wounds and skin grafts. Our prayers now were focused on the healing of Tom's wounds, and continued strength and courage to face the intensive rehabilitation that lay ahead.

> *[Tom] Dave, the occupational therapist, now had me sitting at the edge of my bed, without back support, for my meals. Trying to eat (but not wanting to) with a tray table positioned in front of me in case I started to fall out of bed— what a combination.*

> *One day Dave announced that he wanted me to stand by myself next to the bed. (I never know when these things are coming.) He had been doing some exercises with me sitting at the side of the bed with my legs dangling over the side, then he just announced that he was going to have me stand. In comes a walker and they set it in front of me.*

> *I can't remember if Dave got me off the bed or if there was another person there helping, but I remember worrying that my bad leg would just collapse and tear apart. In reality, that was the least of my worries. Yes, the leg hurt but it held me up. As the weight went onto my leg, though, it felt like all the bones in my feet cracked. Then my ankle. Then my knees and my hips. All the way up my back to my neck. I thought I was*

going to pass out. I stood for a full 13 seconds (they timed me), but it felt like forever. I think I shrunk three inches with all my bones cracking and compressing. Everyone went nuts, they were so excited, but to me it was pathetic, a terrible attempt on my part.

Much later I learned that Dave didn't know if I'd be able to do it at all, let alone for 13 seconds. He learned that day that if he put a challenge in front of me, I'd do everything I could to meet his goal.

Sunday, August 15

Hooray—Tom was moved to the Burn Unit!

On Friday, Tom sat at the edge of his bed. On Saturday he then slid over to a large "support" chair, and sat there for an hour. He was light-headed, as was to be expected, but he did it. We continue to be impressed by Tom's courage in approaching all of these "new" challenges.

Now that we were in the Burn Unit, Tom's dressing changes could be done by the nursing staff down the hall. This was a whole new experience for both of us.

> *[Tom] Soon after getting moved, two nurses come in my room to take me down the hall for my wound cleaning. On this floor, there is a special area used for debriding and cleaning burn wounds. In ICU this had been done right in my room because I couldn't be moved. Now all I could think of were the horror stories I'd heard about burn victim treatments. I'm thinking it must be like a torture chamber—and Sue won't be there for the first time. She was always with me downstairs and would talk me through and let me squeeze her hand when it hurt the most. I am very nervous and can barely answer when the nurses ask me questions.*

> *We enter the room pushing my gurney through a wide door. There are a couple of stainless steel whirlpool tanks, stainless steel tables, and curtain dividers everywhere. I am pulled*

onto a stainless steel table wearing just my thin hospital gown. They start to remove my bandages and instead of the freezing cold I expect, I feel radiant heat. I think it was coming from the ceiling, but I'm not sure. They start rinsing my wound and the water is warm. No shivers at all. Here they can give me an (almost) full bath for the first time in a month. It feels good and so much easier than being bathed in bed.

I am taken back to my room where Sue awaits in anticipation. The nurses fill her in on the procedure—one of the first she hadn't witnessed since I had been hospitalized. Sue says it is a relief for her not to have to sit through this, but at the same time hard not to be there to help and to see the progress of my healing.

My room is very quiet. I barely have any machines in my room and the nurse's desk is way down the hall from my room, not just outside my door like in the ICU. There are very few patients in the Burn Unit ward right now, but the nurses oversee many patients instead of just one or two. The nurses stop in to check on me less often than when I was downstairs.

I think I feel a little nervous not being constantly checked on by the doctors and nurses.

It is very quiet—almost lonely, actually.

Another new, troubling problem was that Tom was breaking into sweats off and on throughout the day and night. The hospital staff told us it could be related to the reduction in pain medications—in other words, drug withdrawal. They were switching to a different combination of pain meds and sedatives in the Burn Unit—ones that are better for controlling skin and wound pain. Tom was down to wearing 125 mg Fentanyl patches, plus a dose of Versed or Vicodin preceding dressing changes; still a lot, but less than what he had been getting.

Wednesday, August 18
(Three days later)

Baby steps—literally! Tom took his first two baby steps on Monday. With a therapist on either side, holding on to a walker, and groaning in pain, he took two baby steps forward and then three more backwards to his bed.

We were thrilled but Tom was discouraged. He was frustrated by how weak and dysfunctional his body was. We watched in amazement at how he was able to do more on his own each day, but he couldn't see the overall progress like we could. It was a struggle for me to find the balance between being a tough-love coach and an empathetic spouse.

Tom could now shimmy himself over onto a gurney bed which was his transport to the room down the hall. He finally had enough control over his legs to be able to reposition them himself—another small, but big accomplishment.

Tom's right arm and hand were quite functional now, but the therapists discovered that his left arm was severely hindered by a "frozen shoulder." He couldn't lift his left arm any higher than his chest. The therapists rigged up a pulley contraption over Tom's bed so he could do exercises to begin loosening his shoulder joint. Tom said it looks like something from the Three Stooges. He expected to pull on it and get snapped in the face. *Now, there's something to look forward to.*

[Tom] Within a few days they had me walking with the walker short distances across my room, then to the door, and eventually out into the hall. As I was still wearing only a hospital gown, a second gown would be draped over my shoulders to cover my backside. We joked about it being my superhero cape.

As much as I wanted to walk and be back to normal, it was frightening. Walking hurt and the pain made me sick to my stomach. What if I fall, won't it tear my leg apart? If I start walking more, I will have to leave the safety of the hospital and I'm not ready to go home . . . I was losing the security of my bed.

I got over half way down the hall, and then made it back to my room. I think everyone who worked on that floor was watching and cheering. It seemed like it took forever. All I did was shuffle. I couldn't get my legs to pick my feet up off the ground. It was exciting and painful and nauseating.

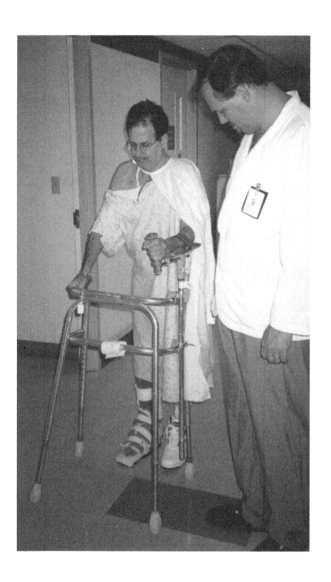

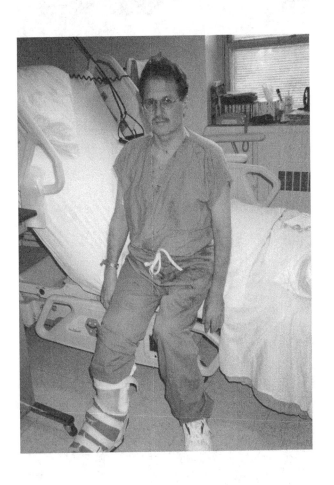

As Tom was working to overcome these physical limitations, I couldn't help but think of the many, many elderly or disabled individuals who struggle with these simple tasks on a daily basis—with no hope of improvement. I now understood their struggles in a new way and realized how important it is to remember these individuals in our prayers, to offer them support and encouragement. They deserve to be treated with patience, dignity, and respect. I will forever be impressed by the courage and tenacity shown by individuals who live with long-term disabilities of any kind.

We were excited to learn that the last treatment areas, the open wounds just above his hip, were finally ready to be closed. The surgeon had scheduled this FINAL reconstructive surgery for first thing tomorrow morning. I was thrilled. Tom was again, understandably, apprehensive.

Thursday, August 19

Even before Tom entered surgery, I was reminded of how much he had improved. This time we had to follow the regular surgery routine like everyone else.

I had become accustomed to staying with Tom in his ICU room until the very last minute before they whisked him down the hall directly into the operating room. Today, I woke up early, drove to the hospital, and arrived 45 minutes before his scheduled surgery only to find they had wheeled him from his room ten minutes earlier.

I found Tom downstairs in the pre-op area along with the rest of the regular surgery patients. When they took him away to surgery a short time later, instead of waiting in a private room until he returned, Tom's mother and I sat in the surgical waiting room with the other 10-20 families waiting for surgeons to deliver their post-op reports. We then waited another hour until Tom came out of recovery before we could see him. Kind of odd to have a normal surgery routine seem so unfamiliar to us.

Even though I knew Tom was in good hands, I couldn't help but worry about how he was doing without us next to him. I was accustomed to being intimately involved in everything about his medical care. I felt an unexpected disconnect. I felt like I had been pushed aside. *Ah well, . . . small price to pay for improved stability.*

Surgery went well. As expected, they grafted the two remaining areas near his right hip using skin from Tom's outer right thigh. They used a general anesthesia through a mask and did not have to intubate him. Later in the day he ate a little bit of supper, but then felt queasy afterwards. Tom was very tired and felt lousy all day, but that was to be expected. We hoped he could get a good night's rest and that his appetite would improve again tomorrow.

Because of the surgery, Tom had a day off from physical therapy, but they would probably have him up walking again in the morning. As much as the therapy hurt, and as frustrated as Tom was by his inability to walk and function independently, it was one of the few things in his life that he could influence or control right now. He was motivated to work hard. He wanted to get HOME as soon as possible.

Sunday, August 22

They decided to hold off on walking for a few more days. Part of the new graft crossed over the top of Tom's leg where it bent, so they wanted to make sure the skin graft wouldn't pull away. It was frustrating for him to be stuck in bed again after getting some mobility this past week. At the same time he didn't mind putting off more pain and suffering for another day or two.

In spite of his immobility, Tom's appetite improved—or at least the amount that he ate increased. He knows that the more he eats, the better equipped his body will be to heal. The better he eats, the sooner he'll get rid of the feeding tube and eventually get back home.

Friday night, we'd had a movie-dinner in Tom's room with the boys. The kids picked out a movie (Karate Kid) and brought cafeteria tray meals up to Tom's room where we ate together while watching the video. It was the most time we'd spent together as a family in almost two months. We all enjoyed it, but it was still rather strange and sad . . .

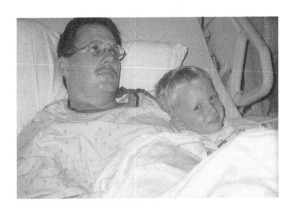

Monday, August 23

The staff told us that the latest skin grafts were looking great. (We had an interesting discussion with the Burn Unit nurse reminding her that what looked "great" to them looked pretty hideous to the rest of us—but we would take their word for it and be thankful.)

Tom was once again walking down the hall and back. Very slowly. With a walker. But, hey, he was on the move.

With summer at an end, the boys would be starting school tomorrow. Once again, family and friends stepped up and picked up all the boys' school supplies to get them ready for the new year. What a huge help to us.

My classes would be starting at Aquinas this week as well. I was taking a semester off from my master's program but was scheduled to teach on Tuesday's and Friday's, just two half-days each week. Part of me was eager to get back to life outside of the hospital, even though I knew it would be a struggle to find time for everything.

We continued to post updates online on Tom's progress. We asked for prayers focused on Tom's quick and complete recovery—specifically for healing of the pressure sore on his right heel, two small skin graft areas on his calf that had not closed, medial nerve problems in both hands, and continued strength and flexibility in his legs.

Monday, August 30
(a week later)

Although Tom made good progress over the past seven days, the week ended up being quite a challenge.

When Tom was first hospitalized, another friend of ours, Don Condit, would stop by Tom's room regularly and check Tom's hands and feet for complications resulting from the high doses of pressor drugs. Don was an orthopedic doctor who specialized in hands and wrists. When Tom could finally move his limbs on his own, Don recommended that Tom be tested for possible nerve damage.

The staff ordered an EMG (electromyogram) test to gauge nerve responses to electrical impulses in his extremities. The testing was done in the neurology testing lab of what seemed like the basement of the hospital. They brought Tom down in a wheelchair but then transferred him to a gurney for the procedure. *(Of course, I went along to watch.)*

When we arrived at the lab, the technician hooked up electrodes to Tom's hands and arms and plugged them into a control box. The neurologist sat with his back to us carefully reading the displays and adjusting the control knobs and settings. As the first few shocks didn't register any effect at all, the doctor cranked up the dials. When they administered the next electric shock, Tom all but flipped right off his gurney. (*"Just like Dead Man Walking,"* Tom said.)

The testing lasted for 20-30 minutes and was not a particularly pleasant experience for Tom. In the end, the results indicated definite compression of the median nerve in Tom's wrist, damage which most likely occurred as a result of the pressor drugs and retention of over 100 lbs. of extra fluid. This meant that Tom would need carpal tunnel surgery on his wrist to relieve the pressure.

Then, later in the week, Tom started running a fever. As his white blood count was elevated, they ordered additional tests mid-week to rule out any new, serious problems. They took an x-ray of his frozen shoulder, took blood, urine, and IV cultures, and did an ultrasound on his leg to rule out the possibility of a blood clot. *Yikes— déjà vu.*

The x-rays on his shoulder confirmed adhesions in the joint causing Tom's "frozen shoulder." This would require additional physical therapy but no additional procedures. Thankfully, all of the other test results came back negative.

They removed the PICC line in Tom's upper arm (used for IV's and blood draws) since it presented a possible infection site. In its place they inserted a simple IV line in his forearm. They also *finally* removed the Dobhoff feeding tube this week.

> *[Tom] A nurse I had never seen before came in this morning and told me she was going to remove my feeding tube. They think I'm finally getting enough calories and I don't need it any*

more. She takes all the tape off my face and disconnects the tubes from the bag. Then she tells me that the faster she does this, the shorter the discomfort will last. My nose will bleed a little, but then it will be over.

She hands me a damp wash cloth and has me lay back against my pillow, holding the wash cloth under my nose. Then she stands next to the bed, grabs the tube close up to my nose, says "Are you ready?" and then . . . Zip. She pulls the tube out so fast that I only feel a quick tug on my stomach and in an instant the 3-foot long tube is out. All these weeks of inserting and adjusting feeding tubes only to have them leak into my hair at night . . . and in a fraction of a second it was all over.

My eyes are watering and my nose is running and bleeding a little, but I'm laughing hysterically. It was the most comical thing I had experienced this whole time. The nurse started cracking up right along with me. "Oh yeah, I told you I was fast!" she laughed. Then she was gone and I never saw her again.

Wow. What a relief. No more tape on my face. No more tubes coming out of my nose. They still would hook me up to a heart monitor at night, but otherwise I was no longer connected to ANY tubes, pumps, bags, or machines. What an amazing feeling of freedom and independence.

Tom was a free man and getting more mobile. By the end of the week not only did he walk down the hallway and back a few times, but, under the close supervision of an OT and PT, he made it up and down a half-flight of stairs. *Wow.*

The worst of the week, however, came on Sunday, and it was an absolute nightmare.

On Friday, they had started Tom on a new drug (Celexa). He started feeling lousy on Saturday morning, but we didn't think too much of it because breakfast didn't arrive until 30-40 minutes after he'd taken his vitamins and morning pills. (*Yuck.*) But by late morning on Sunday, Tom was really feeling awful. He was queasy and unsettled and was getting anxious and extremely fidgety.

[Tom] For the past couple of days I had been feeling restless and uncomfortable and I seemed to be sweating all the time even though sometimes I felt hot and sometimes I felt chilled. This day I felt especially restless. I couldn't seem to relax or get comfortable.

When Susan arrived she was concerned about how profusely I was sweating and checked with the nursing staff to make sure I wasn't running a temperature. No, no fever.

As the day went on I felt more and more restless and anxious. I was exhausted but couldn't sleep.

I couldn't concentrate enough to read. I couldn't even watch TV—the noise was too irritating.

I felt like I needed to move my arms and legs, so I started rocking back and forth in the bed. It was like having what I call crazy legs—where you feel like you HAVE to move your legs— except that my whole body felt like this. One hundred times worse. Including my brain. I felt like if I stopped thrashing I would absolutely lose my mind.

I tried to let it go and relax, but it had a hold over me. I wanted to curl up in a ball and shut down while at the same time it felt like I needed to jump right out of my skin. I felt like I was screaming on the inside.

Susan checked back with the hospital staff to see if any new drugs had been added or changed. She found one new medication and requested that the staff check with the pharmacy for possible side effects. The staff, however, didn't seem too concerned.

By now I was constantly thrashing all over the bed or as much as I could with limited strength and mobility. By now I had stripped most of the bedding off my bed and my pillows were soaked.

As I was still bedridden, I couldn't get up to walk it off. It was driving me crazy. I was trapped in bed, losing my mind. What had been slowly building for days now had me totally in its grip. I was agitated and overwhelmed with feelings of anxiety. I couldn't concentrate on anything. I only knew that Susan was trying to find a solution and that gave me some hope.

Susan was asking now if I might be having withdrawal symptoms as we knew they had been reducing my pain medications. Again, the staff didn't seem to have answers but didn't seem too concerned either.

I was exhausted and Susan was worried. I continued to thrash around as if I was trying not to drown. I felt like something might suck me away if I wasn't careful. I tried to stay focused on the here and now, but it wasn't easy.

Finally, later in the evening, one of the doctors prescribes something for me. Slowly, slowly my body begins to relax. Finally I am able to sleep and rest.

We never could confirm whether Tom had a rare, adverse side effect to the Celexa or if he was suffering serious drug withdrawal from being taken off morphine. For 2-3 hours he was restless and *extremely* agitated—thrashing, moaning, writhing around his bed . . . He felt and acted like he was going out of his mind. We actually had to line both sides of the bed with pillows so he wouldn't hurt himself. It was awful. The hospital staff finally gave him some medication to counteract the reaction he was having and, after a few more hours, he eventually settled down, but it was a nightmare to endure.

Believe it or not, it was one of the worst things we'd had to experience in this ordeal so far.

I surrendered, exhausted and out of alternatives, begging God for protection and strength.

> *"Find rest, O my soul, in God alone; my hope comes from him. He alone is my rock and my salvation; He is my fortress, I will not be shaken." Psalm 62: 5-6 (NIV)*

Tuesday, August 31

An overnight miracle . . . I arrived at the hospital the next day to learn that plans were underway for Tom to move to a rehab facility. Finally, moving day! We didn't know exactly when or how, but sometime tomorrow, Tom would be moved to Mary Free Bed Hospital, an excellent rehabilitation hospital right in downtown Grand Rapids.

I was ecstatic, but Tom was (understandably) apprehensive about moving. Tom's very life had depended upon the medical staff here at this hospital, and now he would have to leave. Progress was good, but it was also scary.

A good portion of the day was spent in preparation for the move—reviewing leg care, outpatient plans, etc.— but most of the day was taken up by one last surgical procedure. The carpal tunnel surgery was needed to relieve the pressure on Tom's left wrist that was pinching the nerves to his hand. We hoped that this would allow the nerves to heal and help improve his fine motor skills.

The surgery, Tom's ninth, went well. They didn't need to use general anesthesia, so he was awake and comfortable shortly after the procedure. Since he couldn't put pressure on his wrist, they switched Tom from a walker to a simple support crutch. The splint on his left arm would need to stay wrapped and dry for two weeks, however, so that did present a slight setback. Tom had just started showering and washing by himself, now he would need help once again. *A small price to pay for progress.*

Wednesday, September 01

Seven weeks ago, we brought Tom into the emergency room. After over 4 weeks in ICU, five debridement surgeries, three skin graft surgeries, plus wrist surgery (just yesterday), Tom was discharged from the hospital today and moved on to another hospital for rehabilitation.

Leaving this hospital was emotional for both of us. Tom only remembers the past three weeks here, but I remember all seven—quite vividly. We made many new friends and found much love and support here. We witnessed the power of prayer and experienced the comforting arms of the Holy Spirit. I have mixed emotions, but no choice and no doubts . . . It is time to move on.

> *[Tom] I remember being very emotional about leaving Blodgett Hospital to move to Mary Free Bed. I had spent nearly two months at Blodgett and was familiar with all the doctors, nurses, and caregivers. Now I would be going somewhere with a whole new staff and an unknown routine. On top of that, it was unknown how long I would need to be in rehab. I remember my doctors telling me I might be at the rehab hospital for 2-4 weeks, after which I might move to a long-term care facility. It all sounded daunting and depressing.*
>
> *I was transferred to Mary Free Bed on a gurney by ambulance. Sue went ahead by car and*

was waiting in my room with the staff when I arrived.

The first thing they did was a case assessment. They measured my leg in several places so they could monitor any swelling. They asked questions about my leg and what the processes were for changing the bandages. Susan had brought wound care supplies from the hospital and explained the daily routine for caring for my leg and other wound sites.

Following this, they had me sit on the edge of the bed and told me to try to get myself to the wheelchair and then into the bathroom. This surprised me as I had always been pushed in the wheelchair and never had to move it myself. I still had a cast on my arm from the carpal tunnel surgery and didn't know if I could even do what they were asking.

While at the hospital, I had learned to use a walker and crutch with one arm, but I didn't know how to move a wheelchair. I was very nervous. My brain was still fuzzy and I didn't realize they were just assessing what I could and couldn't do. I took this as something I was expected to be able to do, so I tried—repeatedly, with limited success. They were watching and taking notes and I felt anxious and frustrated, scared to fail. It never occurred to me that it would be okay if I could NOT do these tasks.

The next assessment was to see if I could shower myself. I had to get to the bathroom in the corner of the room by wheelchair, then stand up and take off all my clothes (aka pajamas). It seemed I had a whole crowd of people watching me, two with clipboards, while I went through this process. Then they had me do it again.

I thought these people were crazy. I thought I was the only sane one in the bunch and couldn't understand why they wanted me to go through all these embarrassing tasks right now, while they watched, when I could hardly do these things at all. In reality, I was the foggy-headed one. I'm sure they explained to me what was happening and why I was doing this, but I was not processing what they were saying.

Eventually I ended up in the hallway with a walker so they could assess my mobility skills. The physiatrist in charge of my case was there watching while I did laps around the floor. (Okay, probably just halfway and back.) The doctor was talking with Susan about my case and treatment plan. I couldn't hear what he was saying but it sounded like a long story.

After finishing my "lap" with the walker, I made it over to where they were standing and asked the doctor when I could leave. He looked at me and smiled and told me that if I can walk to the very end of the hall and turn the corner to the next hall, I could go home Labor Day—in less than a week—but that I would have to do it without a walker and without holding the rail along the wall.

In typical fashion, I rose to the challenge and started shuffling down the hall with Susan and the doctor close behind. When a doctor or staff member would ask me to do something just to test my limits, I interpreted this as confidence in me that I could do it, and I met their bluff. I'm not sure how long it took me to get to the end of the hall and around the corner, but I did it.

Great news for me, but maybe not such great news for Sue. The school year had just started and Sue had already returned to teaching part-time at Aquinas. These were busy weeks and I think she had planned on me being kept busy and cared for at the rehab hospital for a few weeks. Now those short-term plans were out the window. This may have worried Sue but it just inspired me to work harder and prove myself so I could get back home.

My first full day of rehab was like a school day. The first hour of the day staff members went through the hallways collecting patients and bringing them downstairs for therapy. Almost all of us were in wheelchairs and many of the patients were pretty young. I thought there would be primarily older, stroke victims and a few younger accident victims, but it was the opposite. There were many young people with head and neck injuries from car and motorcycle accidents. There were even several gunshot victims.

The therapy room was bright and clean, full of activity. There was a stack of mats on the floor and numerous tables and chairs setup as therapy stations. I was wheeled over to one of the tables where an occupational therapist sat with a tray in front of her. The tray had bowl shape areas, like an oversized mancala game. In some of the bowls were buttons, paperclips, washers, and other small objects. The therapist introduced herself and then explained that she wanted me to pickup three objects from one bowl and move them to another—first with my right hand and then with my left. I wondered why they were wasting my time on such a silly task when what I was really there for was to improve my walking.

I tried first with my right hand but found that I couldn't pick up a single button. Every time I tried I either got nothing or a whole bunch of buttons at once. I told myself that this was probably because I had just had carpal tunnel surgery on this wrist, so I tried with my left hand. Just as bad. My finger tips were numb and I hadn't even realized it. My fine motor skills were awful.

We continued with more fine motor skill activities and then moved on to large muscle therapy. I pushed myself over to a large square table covered with mats that was about coffee table height. This height made it easy to transfer out of my wheelchair and onto the table.

While lying flat on my back, the physical therapist moved my arms and legs measuring my range of motion. I assumed they would be working only on my bad leg but they checked both arms and legs. I was amazed by how stiff my whole body was—not just my bad leg. It felt like my joints were cracking and breaking. It felt like my muscles and tendons would have to tear apart before I could get a normal range of motion back.

Eventually they wheeled me back to my room and encouraged me to rest. The room was very quiet compared to the other hospital and a nap sounded great. I fell asleep instantly. It wasn't long, however, before they came back to get me for another round of therapy. I was to have four therapy sessions every day—exhausting.

Over the next couple of days I had many therapy sessions. It seemed they were always doing something different. They tested my reaction time, my visual tracking, my memory, etc. As I was in the therapy room I started to notice the other patients more. Many had traumatic head injuries or strokes. It was obvious that these patients' abilities were far behind mine even compared to when I first arrived at this rehab hospital. It struck me, though, that they always seemed to be able to smile. The therapists frequently got patients to laugh and would cheer when someone accomplished a new challenge. I would have thought this would be a sad, depressing place but it wasn't. The atmosphere was positive and filled with hope.

While at Mary Free Bed, my wardrobe greatly expanded. Sue brought me new pajama-type pants that tied at the waist (since I couldn't do buttons), some boxers, and t-shirts. I didn't realize at first that switching to "real" clothes was another one of their tricky ways to evaluate me. Once Sue brought in the clothes, the staff watched me try to put everything on, taking note of what I could and could not do on my own. As simple as these clothes were, it was a huge process getting dressed. Socks were extremely difficult and I'm not sure I ever mastered those on my own. Tying shoes wasn't working well at all so we just switched to slip-on shoes instead. They taught me some interesting tips and gave me some handy tools to help. Even though it was frustrating, it was all very practical.

Eventually, practicing getting dressed was extended to first lying in bed in my pajamas with the covers on all the way. This sounds pretty trivial but it was very difficult. Just getting the blankets on and off with my leg in a brace, still wrapped in bandages from ankle to hip, was hard. Now imagine this with partially paralyzed limbs. I had to show the therapists that I could get the blankets off me, get myself out of bed, stand with a cane or walker, re-make the bed, fetch my clothes and carry them into the bathroom, take off all my clothes, pretend to take a shower, and get dressed . . . All without assistance (if possible).

Another evaluation session was in a fake apartment they have built in the occupational therapy area. We went first to the kitchen area. There I was given the task of making a grilled cheese sandwich and pouring myself a glass of milk. Again, easy for me in the past, but not so easy anymore. This challenge required me to open the refrigerator and carry a gallon of milk from the 'fridge to the counter (while walking with my crutch). I then had to get out the butter, bread, cheese, a frying pan and cooking spray. Once everything was out I had to go through all the steps to make the sandwich and pour my drink. Once finished cooking, I then had to clean up after myself. All of this I had to do while balancing on my crutch with one arm still in a brace from my carpal tunnel surgery. Not easy at all.

Another time I was directed to sit on all different types of furniture—straight chairs, cushy chairs, big recliners . . . I found that, once sitting, I couldn't get myself back up out of most of the furniture. But, again, they showed me some tricks, like how to scoot to the edge of the chair before trying to stand up.

One time they even made me lie down right on the floor and then taught me how to get myself back up using nearby furniture. After a bunch of rolling around and some limited success, I did it. Next they had me open and close, lock and unlock the apartment front door. Another time I practiced getting in and out of a "car" they had indoors, an extended part of the "apartment." Since my leg didn't bend very well yet, we were thankful we'd have the minivan instead of a little compact car.

In those first few days I made great progress. I was exhausted but I was regaining range of motion and muscle control. I had fewer visitors but I wasn't in my room much and when I was in my room, I was catching a much-needed nap.

One day they brought me outside and had me practice getting in and out of a minivan (since that is what Sue drove). They showed me how to get from the wheelchair onto the floor of the van and then lift myself onto the seat, pushing up with my good leg. They helped me once or twice and then I tried it on my own. I pulled myself up with my arm, but somehow my bad leg got stuck underneath me and I collapsed falling onto my bad leg, I was in excruciating pain and was completely stuck. I was helpless. They quickly *helped me up, and although my leg hurt, it was fine. Still, I was devastated. I thought that I was becoming so independent and then in a flash I was helpless again. It was a disappointing reality check to see how weak and dependent I still was.*

The evenings at the rehab hospital were pretty quiet. Most patients were exhausted from the day's therapy sessions. Family and friends would stop by for awhile after dinner but then they would go home to leave us to rest. I found that I was exhausted but often couldn't sleep.

My sleep patterns had been disrupted and I would stay awake worrying. I remember wondering if I was ever going to be able to do some of the tasks they were teaching me so I could get home.

I still couldn't concentrate enough to read or follow a movie or TV show. The only thing that seemed to work was silently saying repetitive prayers like the rosary. Through those prayers I would meditate and slowly turn over all my concerns to God. Eventually I would fall into a peaceful sleep.

After a couple of days, the staff visited our house to see if it would be a safe environment for me to return to or not. They recommended changes such as hand rails on the stairs and gained a better understanding of the skills I needed to master before moving back home. Once I was ready, and after any safety issues had been addressed, I would be able to make a day visit back to the house. This would be my biggest test yet.

Ralph, a talented carpenter and longtime family friend, made the recommended safety modifications—an added railing on the stairs, a detachable sprayer in the shower, etc. Without hesitation, Ralph came right over to the house and took care of everything within a day. The house was ready for my test run.

The day of the visit was a beautiful summer afternoon. The hospital staff escorted me via wheelchair to the main entrance where Sue was waiting with the minivan. We loaded me, my crutch, and my wheelchair into the van and off we went on our three-hour pass.

Being out of the hospital was great but it did make me nervous and anxious. I hadn't ridden in a car for almost two months. It felt so odd. Sue sensed my anxiety and thought I was being critical about the way she was driving. I guess we were both feeling a little uptight about this step.

We arrived home and I waddled my way into the house. We decided it would be best not to have the boys around for this first visit, so it was just Sue and me. I couldn't believe how great it was to see the inside of a real house again—especially my own.

I worked my way around the first floor of the house going in the front door, then through the kitchen and into the living room. Suddenly I was overwhelmed by it all, remembering the last time I was home sitting on the couch in pain. I started crying. I could have died . . . !?! Susan started crying too, and we just cried onto each others' arms for a long time.

Eventually we composed ourselves and turned our focus to the task at hand. We needed to see if I could get around the house so I could come back home for good.

Thanks to Ralph's sturdy railings and my support crutch, I was able to safely make it upstairs to our bedroom and bath and back down again. It took a very long time, but I did it. We relaxed on the couch for awhile, but all too soon it was time to go back to the hospital. I was exhausted, but was thrilled to know that I could be coming home again soon—for good.

Over the next few days back at Mary Free Bed, the staff worked hard to get me ready to go home. They taught me exercises to do at home for fine motor skills, leg mobility and upper body strength. At this point I had to do all the exercises lying down instead of upright because I was still too weak to fight gravity AND do the exercises at the same time. But I was willing to work hard. They sketched out an outpatient schedule for physical therapy visits and rented a wheelchair for me to use so I could get to and from outpatient therapy.

Finally the day came . . . Labor Day weekend, on Sunday, September 5th, I moved home.

The hospital staff helped Sue pack up all my belongings and they wheeled me out to the car. Surprisingly, I was not scared to leave the hospital this time, just nervous and excited.

When we arrived at the house, Sue helped me out of the car and made me stop at the front door so she could take my picture. Our family had put up decorations on the outside and inside, in the kitchen. But very quickly I was overcome with emotion. I made it to the family room where I collapsed and started to cry and shake. Sue joined me on the couch and together we had another good cry. We couldn't believe I'd made it home.

Over the next few days we fell into a new routine. I learned how to get around the house and deal with basic tasks and Sue developed a system for tracking my new symptoms and medications. As my medical care was still pretty significant, life was not back to normal by any means.

Once a day Sue had to check my wounds, unwrap my bandages, and help me into the shower. The wounds on my leg hurt all the time but they were especially painful when exposed to the air. When I was finished showering, I dried off and Sue re-bandaged all my wounds. The process was very painful for me and a challenge for Sue. Without a raised hospital bed and an extra person to help, it was hard to keep everything dry and wrap my leg quickly. Each time we got a little better, but we were both physically and emotionally exhausted by the time I was back on the couch.

The boys came home on Monday, Labor Day. They were so excited to have us all home again.

The next day would be Sue's 40th birthday so the boys arrived home with a cake and a gift for their mom. I propped myself up on the couch while Sue sat at my feet with the boys, and we had an impromptu party right there with just the five of us.

Over the next few days, each of the boys took turns beating their mom at Nintendo Mario

Cart—the present they'd picked out for Sue—while I rested nearby on the couch.

It felt so good to be a family again.

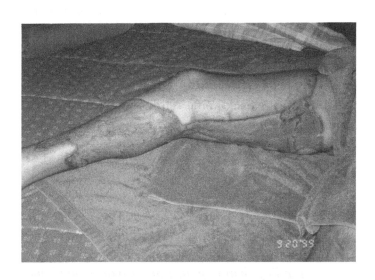

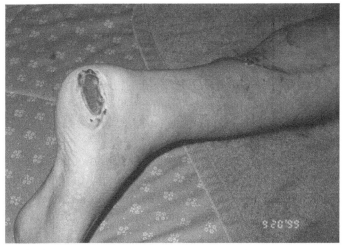

November 1999

We were thankful to be home, but it wasn't easy. For a time, in September, I had four "boys" demanding my time and attention. It would take a very long time before Tom was more of a husband and father than a patient.

Our first weeks back home reminded me of when we brought home our first newborn—lots of anxiety and second-guessing. It was a very stressful and exhausting time. Again, we had to cling to our faith to sustain us.

> *"Cast all your anxiety on him because He cares for you. Be self-controlled and alert. Your enemy the devil prowls around like a roaring lion, looking for someone to devour. Resist him, standing firm in your faith, because you know that your brothers throughout the world are undergoing the same kind of sufferings. And the God of all grace, who called you to his eternal glory in Christ, after you have suffered a little while, will himself restore you and make you strong, firm, and steadfast. To him be the power for ever and ever. Amen." I Peter 5:7-11 (NIV)*

In October, Tom started going to a friend of ours, John Dery, for physical therapy. John, had Tom not only exercising, but also doing occupational therapy by washing dishes, folding laundry, etc. *I loved this guy!*

Recovery was not without its setbacks, however, Tom struggled with a great deal of pain, he was suffering from circulatory problems in his extremities, his blood pressure and heart rates were too high, and he wasn't sleeping well. On top of everything else, he developed shingles!

Tom kept pushing ahead, though, and by mid-November he even started driving. First he would just drive to physical therapy sessions and back, but soon he started driving to work in the afternoons. By late November he was working almost full-time and his blood pressure had stabilized without the continual need for medication. *Hallelujah!*

Through it all, I continued to wonder, *was this a miracle?* Many people, doctors included, think it was. Was Tom's life spared because of the prayers of so many? In the Bible, there are many examples of God "changing" his plans because of people's intercessory pleas. But, I certainly hesitated to make that assumption with Tom. Maybe God planned it to happen this way all along. I suppose, it doesn't matter exactly how or why Tom's life was spared. What did matter was that God had reached down and touched many of us deeply through this experience. For that we would be eternally grateful and honored.

This experience, for me, reinforced the importance of building a personal relationship with God and of being an active member of a faith community—***before*** we face a crisis. Although God will welcome us at any time, we will be less prepared to handle the situation and will not have the same kind of support network if we don't nurture our faith ahead of time. Not unlike training for a marathon or some other major athletic competition, we need to put the time and effort into preparing for the event before it happens. If we invest in our relationship with God and make Him a priority when times are good, we will be better prepared to receive His graces when faced with times of trouble. Jesus tells us:

> *"Therefore everyone who hears these words of mine and puts them into practice is like a wise man who built his house upon the rock. The rain came down, the streams rose, and the winds blew and beat against that house; yet it did not fall, because it had its foundation on the rock. But everyone who hears these words of mine and does not put them into practice is like a foolish man who built his house on sand. The rain came down, the streams rose, and the winds blew and beat against that house, and it fell with a great crash." Matthew 7:24-27 (NIV)*

Now that we had made it through this crisis, would we be able to keep God as the central, focal point of our lives?

> *"Do not store up for yourselves treasures on earth, where moths and vermin destroy, and where thieves break in and steal. But store up for yourselves treasures in heaven, where moths and vermin do not destroy, and where thieves do not break in and steal. For where your treasure is, there your heart will be also." Matthew 6:19-21 (NIV)*

June 2000—MS150 Bike Ride

[Tom] Throughout my hospital stays and my rehab, all my various caregivers picked up on the fact that I like to ride my bike. They would use biking as incentive to get me to work harder.

I remember Sue first using it when I was getting my wounds cleaned and re-bandaged. The procedures were excruciating. Sue would let me hold and squeeze her hand to deal with the pain. She would talk me through it by describing a long, hard bike ride or riding up a hill. She would tell me where I was on the climb, my progress up the hill, and when I was near the peak she would tell me I needed to give it one last bit of energy to make it over the top. Then the procedure would be over.

The staff, especially the physical therapists, would use my passion for riding to encourage and inspire me. At first the challenge of just bending my leg was with the goal of someday being able to ride again. Eventually biking became part of my actual therapy.

When I started going to our friend John Dery for physical therapy, he really ramped up my use of stationary bikes. He had a nice Schwinn AirDyne bike at his office that exercised your arms and legs at the same time. At first I could only pedal a half a rotation and even then it felt like my leg was going to snap off. Before I could complete one full pedal cycle with my legs, I would use my arms to finish up the rotation. Over time, as my muscle strength and flexibility returned, the pedaling motion began to feel more natural. John would leave me to work out on the bike for longer and longer periods of time, monitoring my heart rate and blood pressure for safe cardio conditioning.

Through that first fall and winter, my physical therapy sessions began to taper off and I began exercising more at home. Sue's cousin Tom gave us a nice stationary bike that they were no longer using. We put the bike in the basement and I added it to my prescribed exercise routine along with the elastic bands, leg weights, and arm weights.

By the time spring came, I was able to ride on the stationary bike for 45-60 minutes at a time. It was a great workout and I began to think about the day when I could ride outside again.

One nice day in April, I decided to try. It was still cool, but not cold, perfect weather for biking. My biggest fear was scraping my leg. What would happen if I fell . . . ?!? There was just one thin layer of skin over my calf. Would it all just shred apart and open up? Would I tear the muscles and tendons? Would I get another terrible infection? How would my balance be? Would I be able to get back home if I rode too far? These thoughts kept spinning through my mind, but I headed out anyway.

I wore long biking pants to keep my leg covered. The tight fabric felt good on my skin grafts and gave me some confidence. I wore a heart monitor watch and set the alarm levels to make sure I wouldn't get my heart rate up too high. I packed my cell phone and wallet in my seat pack and headed out.

I had no idea where I was going because I didn't really think I would be going that far. I started down the driveway and up the hill out of the neighborhood. As I was pedaling up the hill I was so nervous that I felt a little nauseous.

Slowly I became aware of how I really felt. It was so much easier than I anticipated. No big exercise bike. No clunky machines. I was actually outside traveling on a bike under my own power! The sensation of speed and freedom made me feel like a little kid again. I just kept riding farther and farther away from home and the smile on my face just kept getting bigger and bigger.

I found myself following one of my old training routes. I was excited to see what it would be like to go down big hills and what it would be like to have to climb back up again.

This wasn't physical therapy. This wasn't exercise training. It was just unbelievably FUN.

It wasn't the fastest I have ever ridden up or down some of these hills, but it FELT twice as fast as before. The effort was just as hard or harder than before I got sick but doubly rewarding. It was easier than I thought it would be. It felt like I had taken off a giant weight suit. It was as if all my physical therapy had been done on a different planet where the gravity was stronger and now all of the sudden the gravitational pull was back to normal. It was as if God said my body was ready and He put me back on Earth.

My hands and feet were getting very cold, so I decided I needed to get back home. It was a problem I'd had since being in the hospital. The circulation to my hands and feet were damaged from the pressor drugs they gave me early on; my hands and feet soon hurt from the cold.

When I finally returned home, Sue was there waiting. I had a huge grin on my face. "Well, how far did you go?" she asked. To her surprise I replied, "Over 20 miles." I couldn't believe it and neither could she. It was the best I had felt in a very long time.

I continued riding outside when the weather was good—learning to keep my hands and feet covered on cooler days. When the weather didn't permit riding outside, I would put in time on the exercise bike in the basement.

As the weeks passed, I began to seriously consider riding in the MS150 ride come June. I had ridden in this two-day tour every year for the past six years and had completed the MS150 most recently just one month before my hospitalization.

Some of my friends who had ridden in past MS150 rides started joining me on my training rides. Ron Webster, the one who first introduced me to this ride, put the word out and would set up times and places for us to ride. We would often go out on Saturday mornings and ride 15-25 miles together. By early June I was ready.

The night before the MS150 ride, I met some of the guys at a local bar. Barth Wilson and Ron Webster presented me with a t-shirt that said "Miracles Do Happen." I wore that shirt on the second day of the ride and still have it to this day.

The route for the first day of the MS150 went from Grand Rapids, through back roads, and ended near Hope College in Holland. The second day of the ride went north from Holland and then wound back to Grand Rapids, ending at Kentwood High School.

We had a good size group riding that year including Ron, Barth, Jerry, Randy, Ed, David, and my brother-in-law Steve. The first day of the ride just a few of us decided to try to do the 100 mile route. (Traditionally the MS150 ride is a two day, 75 mile a day ride, but I am typically one of the "century riders" that completes two 100-mile rides.) Despite the heat, I was wearing my long biking pants to protect my leg. This meant having to field questions from other bikers all day long, but it was worth it to me.

Usually by lunch time I would be feeling pretty tired and ready for a break. This time I wasn't tired at all. I was running on total adrenaline. I knew that not long after the lunch stop would be the turn off for the century loop. I would have to make a decision soon about riding my usual 100 miles or riding just 75 miles this time. I had been through so much physical therapy and training my legs and heart were in pretty good shape by this time, but I was still worried that I wasn't ready to ride 100 miles in a single day, let alone repeat it the next day. Nervous, I had to make myself eat, knowing that I needed the calories.

Shortly after lunch, Barth, Jerry, and I split off from the group to do the century loop. The route has fewer riders on it than the main loop. Going from our large group down to just three of us, we begin clicking off the miles and increasing our speed. We rode in a pace line like we did in the larger group, but focused more on keeping up our speed up and knocking off the miles.

We rotated leaders every few miles and kept each other going with wise cracks and jokes. We had senseless conversations as well as deep discussions. I still couldn't believe I was really doing this ride. Every so often I would question whether or not I could finish given everything

I'd been through the past eleven months, but I kept on riding.

About ten miles from the finish line we came to the final rest stop. Barth and Jerry wanted to stop for a break but I wanted to continue on and just finish. (Normally it would be the other way around and they would be the ones leaving me behind to rest.) Barth and Jerry encouraged me to go on ahead, so I took off toward the finish line.

I was on a mission now to get this over with and must have been going on pure adrenaline. I was riding as fast as or faster than I had been all day.

As I got within a half mile of the finish I went over a railroad track and felt my leg shake. At first I thought the jolt of the bump on the road made my right leg start to shake, but as I stood on my pedals to coast, I realized that I was shaking because I had made it!

I couldn't believe I had just finished riding 100 miles after nearly dying eleven months earlier. I felt GREAT. In my head I was cheering "God is Good!" and "Believe in Miracles!!"

When I was showering a short time later, I looked down at my leg in wonder. I marveled at how well it worked even though it was covered in ugly scars.

That night we had everyone out to the family cottage for a cookout and to celebrate the day. It was great to celebrate with everyone.

At night the riders went back to Hope College to sleep in the dorms and get ready to for our second day of riding. Most of the guys collapsed onto their beds and fell asleep right away, but I couldn't sleep. I kept thinking about having to do this ride again the next day. I tossed and turned; just as I would fall asleep, a train would go by and wake me up again. I felt like this went on all night.

By morning I was exhausted and didn't feel rested at all. Our group met in the cafeteria for breakfast with several hundred other riders. Everyone had mounds of food on their plates, wanting to pack in the calories for another long ride. My tray, however, had very little on it. I was tired and nervous and couldn't eat.

The day was grey and was threatening to rain. We knew, however, that the ride would go on even if it started to rain. Only heavy thunderstorms or tornados would cancel the ride.

After breakfast we changed into our riding gear. I put on my "Believe in Miracles" t-shirt from Barth. I was the only one in our group planning to do the 100 mile ride.

As we rode out, everyone else took turns in the front of the pace line except me. My friends wanted to make sure I had plenty of energy to ride the century loop on my own. This year the split for the century (100-mile) loop was earlier in the ride than usual. This meant that I would be riding most of the day by myself.

As we were nearing the split, the sky became dark and it started to sprinkle. As everyone pulled away and I turned onto the century loop on my own, it began to pour. Giant rain drops pelted me as I rode. If any of the guys were considering staying with me for the extra 25 miles, this changed their mind.

Within a short time I was soaked through to the skin despite wearing a rain jacket. I couldn't see any other riders ahead of or behind me. I was even beginning to wonder if they had called off the ride due to storms and wondered if the drivers sweeping the course had missed me.

When I arrived at the rest stop for lunch, however, a few other riders were there, so I knew the ride was still on. I took a much-needed break but eventually had to get riding again before my muscles got too stiff. It was still drizzling and I was wet and getting chilled. A slight breeze had picked up making it feel even colder.

I rode at a good pace after that, partly to warm up and partly because I wanted to see my friends back at the finish line before they all left for home. Sue had told me she had plans that afternoon and wouldn't be able to be at the finish this time. I was disappointed but knew that she and the boys would be waiting for me at home to celebrate later.

By the time I neared the finish line, I was wet and tired, sweaty and covered with mud and road grime. As I came around the final corner, Sue was there with a huge banner and a large crowd of people. The guys who rode ahead and many of their spouses were all there to celebrate my accomplishment.

I rode up to Sue and practically fell off my bike as I fell into her arms. We all cried and hugged and cheered, emotional from the ride and from the long journey we'd traveled together the past eleven months.

The weather was gloomy and I was exhausted and filthy . . . and it was the best day ever.

Early 2014

It has been almost fifteen years since we nearly lost Tom. Although Tom and I both still bear the scars from his ordeal, we came out of it with a new appreciation for life, faith, family, and friends.

Tom is doing great. He has full mobility and is in excellent health. The scars on his leg and from his trachea remain, but they are more of a badge of courage than anything else. He has no pain and requires no medications other than ones he would have needed by now anyway to control hereditary cholesterol and high blood pressure.

Over time, Tom discovered a few, minor lasting effects from his illness including an on-going hormone imbalance and cognitive processing/memory loss. The cognitive loss is most noticeable when he is trying to quickly recall peoples' names or struggling to remember how to get to places we've been numerous times before. Most likely these are the result of minor brain damage from the massive pressure drugs that Tom needed early in his hospitalization. Thankfully the losses are very minor and easily accommodated.

Ten years ago our family went through another life-changing event. At the age of 44, having just accepted a full-time, tenure-track faculty position requiring that I complete my doctoral degree, I became unexpectedly pregnant and had another child. We had always wanted more children, but seriously thought that opportunity had passed—especially after everything Tom's body had been through. Although the idea of having another child so late in life was scary and overwhelming for a while, in the end things turned out better than we ever expected. We were blessed with another beautiful and healthy son who has brought great joy to our life and strengthened our family bonds.

Tom and newborn T. Benjamin (2004)

The English Family—September 2012
(Left to right) Steve, Mike, Melissa,
Susan, Tom, Joe, and Ben

And so our lives continued on. I finished my Ph.D. and earned tenure at the college. Two of the boys have finished college and moved out of the house. And, in addition to another son, we now have a lovely daughter-in-law, and two beautiful grandchildren.

Life has not been without its challenges and sorrows, but we have remained firm in our faith and our commitment to God and to family. We are thankful for our many blessings—big and small—and continue to look for ways to be a blessing to others.

As I stop and think about what we've been through, it strikes me that everyone, at some time or another, has to face the "valley of the shadow of death" (Psalm 23). When I look at the people around me—family, friends, and strangers on the street—I know that each one of us has our own troubles to face. Real life is not as easy or pretty as the media leads us to believe. Real life is about life and death, sickness and health, joy and sadness. How we deal with these realities is what gives our life definition. It reveals our priorities and values.

I sometimes feel guilty about the amount of support that Tom and I received during this ordeal. We happen to know an unusually large number of people as we are both from this area, Tom is a lifetime member of our parish, and we have both volunteered on countless church committees over the years. Also, because Tom's illness was so sudden and unusual, it got the attention of friends and strangers alike. One lesson learned, I suppose, is that getting involved—especially with a faith-based community—has untold benefits.

The support we received from our family, friends, and parish family was AMAZING. This faith community came together and demonstrated: 1) how powerful prayer can be; and 2) how important it is to help one another in times of need. What is especially beautiful is that this community didn't just respond to Tom and me, they have also helped countless other families and individuals in the years since Tom's illness.

We realize that many people, through no fault of their own, do not have friends and family members available to help them. And many people have burdens to bear that are heavier even than ours were. It is our prayer that by the sharing our story, others will be inspired to get involved with a faith community, and will seek out ways to serve and help one another in times of need.

May the peace of God be with you.

"To him who is able to keep you from falling and to present you before his glorious presence without fault and with great joy—to the only God our Savior be glory, majesty, power, and authority, through Jesus Christ our Lord, before all ages, now and forevermore. Amen." Jude 1:24-25 (NIV)

Appendices

Bible Verses Referenced

". . . Even though I walk through the valley of the shadow of death, I will fear no evil, for you are with me . . ." Psalm 23 (NIV)

"Therefore do not worry about tomorrow, for tomorrow will worry about itself. Each day has enough trouble of its own." Matthew 6:34 (NIV)

"Trust in the Lord with all your heart, and lean not on your own understanding. In all your ways, acknowledge Him and He will direct your paths." Proverbs 3:5-6 (NIV)

"Is any one of you sick? He should call the elders of the church to pray over him and anoint him with oil in the name of the Lord. And the prayer offered in faith will make the sick person well; the Lord will raise him up." James 5:14, 15 (NIV)

"Have no anxiety about anything, but in everything by prayer and supplication with thanksgiving let your requests be made known to God. And the peace of God, which passes all understanding, will keep your hearts and your minds in Christ Jesus." Philippians 4:6,7 (NIV)

"For this reason a man will leave his father and mother and be united to his wife, and they will become one flesh." Genesis 2:24 (NIV)

"In the same way, the Spirit helps us in our weakness. We do not know what we ought to pray for, but the Spirit himself intercedes for us with groans that words cannot express." Romans 8:26 (NIV)

"Abba, Father," He said, "everything is possible for you. Take this cup from me. Yet not what I will, but what you will." Mark 14:36 (NIV)

"I tell you the truth, if anyone says to this mountain, 'Go, throw yourself into the sea,' and does not doubt in his heart but believes that what He says will happen, it will be done for him. Therefore I tell you, whatever you ask for in prayer, believe that you have received it, and it will be yours." Mark 11:23, 24 (NIV)

And it shall come to pass that whoever calls on the name of the LORD shall be saved. Acts 2:21 (NKJV)

"Humble yourselves, therefore, under God's mighty hand, that He may lift you up in due time. Cast all your anxiety on him because He cares for you." I Peter 5:6, 7 (NIV)

"Even youths shall faint and be weary, and young men shall fall exhausted; but they who wait for the Lord shall renew their strength, they shall mount up with wings like eagles, they shall run and not be weary, they shall walk and not faint." Isaiah 40:31 (NIV)

"I can do all things through Christ who strengthens me." Philippians 4:13 (NIV)

"This is the day the Lord has made; let us rejoice and be glad." Psalm 118:24 (NIV)

"Cast all your cares on the Lord and He will sustain you . . ." Psalm 55:22 (NIV)

"For I was hungry and you gave me something to eat, I was thirsty and you gave me something to drink, I was a stranger and you invited me in, I needed clothes, and you clothed me, I was sick and you looked after me, I was in prison and you came to visit me . . . . The King will reply, 'I tell you the truth, whatever you did for one of the least of these brothers of mine, you did for me.'" Matthew 25:35-36, 40 (NIV)

"There is a time for everything, and a season for every activity under heaven." Eccl 3:1 (NIV)

"I am the Lord, the God of all mankind, is anything too hard for me?" Jeremiah 32:27 (NIV)

"Cast all your anxiety on him because He cares for you. Be self-controlled and alert. Your enemy the devil prowls around like a roaring lion, looking for someone to devour. Resist him, standing firm in your faith, because you know that your brothers throughout the world are undergoing the same kind of sufferings. And the

God of all grace, who called you to his eternal glory in Christ, after you have suffered a little while, will himself restore you and make you strong, firm, and steadfast. To him be the power forever and ever. Amen." I Peter 5:7-11 (NIV)

"So do not fear, for I am with you; do not be dismayed, for I am your God.
I will strengthen you and help you; I will uphold you with my righteous right hand."
Isaiah 41:10 (NIV)

". . . though the doors were locked, Jesus came and stood among them and said, "Peace be with you." . . . Thomas said to him, "My Lord and my God!" Then Jesus told him, "Because you have seen me, you have believed; blessed are those who have not seen and yet have believed." John 20:26-29 (NIV)

"Now faith is being sure of what we hope for and certain of what we do not see."
Hebrews 11:1 (NIV)

"However, as it is written: 'No eye has seen, no ear has heard, no mind has conceived what God has prepared for those who love him' but God has revealed it to us by his Spirit. The Spirit searches all things, even the deep things of God."
I Corinthians 2:9-10 (NIV)

"And whatever you do, whether in word or deed, do it all in the name of the Lord Jesus,

giving thanks to God the Father through him."
Colossians 3:17

"Therefore I tell you, do not worry about your life, what you will eat or drink; or about your body, what you will wear. Is not life more important than food, and the body more important than clothes? . . . But seek first his kingdom and his righteousness, and all these things will be given to you as well." Matthew 6:25-33 (NIV)

"O Lord, you have searched me and you know me . . . Where can I go from your Spirit? Where can I flee from your presence? If I go up to the heavens, you are there; if I make my bed in the depths, you are there . . . Search me, O God, and know my heart . . . lead me in the way everlasting." Psalm 139 (NIV)

"Therefore everyone who hears these words of mine and puts them into practice is like a wise man who built his house upon the rock. The rain came down, the streams rose, and the winds blew and beat against that house; yet it did not fall, because it had its foundation on the rock. But everyone who hears these words of mine and does not put them into practice is like a foolish man who built his house on sand. The rain came down, the streams rose, and the winds blew and beat against that house, and it fell with a great crash." Matthew 7:24-27 (NIV)

"To him who is able to keep you from falling and to present you before his glorious presence without fault and with great joy—to the only God our Savior be glory, majesty, power, and authority, through Jesus Christ our Lord, before all ages, now and forevermore. Amen."
Jude 1:24-25 (NIV)

"Children are a gift from the Lord . . . Psalms 127:3

"Find rest, O my soul, in God alone; my hope comes from him. He alone is my rock and my salvation; He is my fortress, I will not be shaken." Psalm 62: 5-6 (NIV)

"Because of this many of his disciples turned back and no longer went about with him. So Jesus asked the twelve, "Do you also wish to go away?" Simon Peter answered him, 'Lord, to whom can we go? You have the words of eternal life. We have come to believe and know that you are the Holy One of God.'" John 6:68 (NIV)

"For I was hungry and you gave me something to eat, I was thirsty and you gave me something to drink, I was a stranger and you invited me in, I needed clothes and you clothed me, I was sick and you looked after me, I was in prison and you came to visit me.' Then the righteous will answer him, 'Lord, when did we see you hungry and feed you, or thirsty and give you something to drink? When did we see you a stranger and invite you in, or needing clothes and clothe you? When did we see you sick or in prison and go to visit you?' The King will reply, 'Truly I tell you, whatever you did for one of the least of these brothers and sisters of mine, you did for me.'" Matthew 25:35-40 (NIV)

About Necrotizing Fasciitis

Necrotizing fasciitis is an aggressive type of bacterial infection that destroys the fascia layer (the white connective tissue between the skin and muscle). The infection is most commonly caused by group A Streptococcus (group A strep), and usually occurs at the site of a cut, scrape, bruise, puncture wound, or surgical incision. Necrotizing fasciitis infections are rare in otherwise healthy people and are seen most often in individuals whose immune systems are already compromised due to diabetes, chemotherapy, autoimmune disorders, and other chronic illnesses. A key symptom is extreme pain that seems out of proportion to the visible injuries.

For more information, explore these websites:

National Necrotizing Fasciitis Foundation (NNFF)
http://www.nnff.org/nnff_factsheet.htm

National Institutes of Health
http://www.nlm.nih.gov/medlineplus/ency/article/001443.htm

Centers for Disease Control and Prevention
http://www.cdc.gov/features/necrotizingfasciitis/

How to Help Yourself

A wise person once said "If you don't take care of yourself, you won't have anything left of you to give to those you love." We know this is true, and, even though it is hard to do, we need to remind ourselves that we can't be of much help to those around us if we aren't taking care of ourselves.

Naturally, "taking care of yourself" means different things to each one of us. For me, it meant eating healthy foods, getting enough sleep, and taking the time to primp just a little—put on makeup, do my hair, and shave my legs.

Here are some specific suggestions to consider:

- Eat healthy and drink more water than you usually do. Vegetables and fruits make excellent quick snacks and will help you feel better overall than junk food or candy bars.

- Keep a medical journal. When the doctors talk, take notes. Write down the date and time. It is okay to ask them to repeat what they've said. It is important to keep track of what is happening so you can be a part of the medical decisions. It also helps you more accurately explain the situation to others (friends or medical personnel) if you have clear notes on what medications or procedures are being prescribed. Without some notes, it is nearly impossible to keep important facts, times, and dates in order.

- Learn names and occupations. Write down and learn the last names of the key medical people you meet. Make note of what their primary specialty is: nursing, dietician, respiratory therapist, cardiologist, etc. Once you have this information, you will be able to ask the right questions of the right people with less likelihood of wasting their time or getting misinformation.

- Keep a personal journal. You may wish to keep a private journal, but it doesn't have to be. It helps to put things down on paper—not just emotional reactions, necessarily, but also the chronology of events. In a crisis, time and events quickly become blurred. By keeping even a factual journal, you will have something to refer back to that will help you put things in perspective. In contrast to the medical journal, this notebook could contain notes on who helped you by bringing meals or stopping to visit, or it could contain random questions and ideas that you need to address in the future. Use it in whatever way makes sense to you, but don't just rely on your memory.

- Find a reliable information source such as a support group that specializes in your situation. Depending upon where you live, you may have local resources available, or you may wish to tap into the many resources on the Internet. (Be very careful about online resources, however, as there are many inadequate sites and an abundance of sites posting inaccurate information. I recommend starting with websites posted by recognized organizations, such as the American Medical Association.)

- Find a way to share information with the people who care about your situation. You could set up a web page, as I did, or you may find that sending email messages or periodically changing your outgoing message on your voice mail or answering machine works well. You may also find someone who could relieve you of this responsibility altogether so that you only have to communicate updates to one person and they take care of telling everyone else.

- Browse good books. You may find comfort reading an inspirational book or devotional. You may prefer to escape temporarily into a fictional novel or comedy movie. Personally, my attention span was too short for any significant reading during our crisis, but I know books were a relief to some of our friends and family.

- Listen to music. There are wonderful music CDs and tapes available. You may find that you enjoy songs with inspirational lyrics or that you prefer orchestral or meditational music with no voices at all. There are also a number of beautiful rosary tapes available. My favorite rosary CD is one by Dana and Fr. Kevin Scallon.—so soothing!

- Escape (temporarily). Take a break from everything once in awhile and shop or "window-shop" at one of your favorite stores. Meet a friend for lunch (even if it is the hospital cafeteria). Splurge on a little treat—something affordable that will make you smile and feel refreshed. I remember buying pretty little notepads and some new makeup—things that I knew I needed, but things that were fresh and new and made me feel good.

- Try to get enough sleep. If you can't get enough sleep because of conditions out of your control, try to make what sleep you can get to be GOOD sleep. Remember that God is in control. He is up to and eager to carry your burdens for you.

Worry Not
by Fr. Walter Farrell, O.P.

Let God tend to the hopeless-looking things. You are a Dominican, a foreigner to worry and quite a close friend of gaiety . . . It seems to me quite entrancing to be able to pile into bed realizing there is someone as big as God to do all the worrying that has to be done.

Worry, you know, is a kind of reverence given to a situation because of its magnitude; how small it must be through God's eyes . . . You can't get everything done in a day, nor can you get any part of it done as well as it could be, or even as well as you'd like it; so, like the rest of us, you putter at your job with a normal amount of energy, for a reasonable length of time, and go to bed with the humiliating yet exhilarating knowledge that you are only a child of God and not God Himself.

"Do not be anxious about anything, but in every situation, by prayer and petition, with thanksgiving, present your requests to God. And the peace of God which transcends all understanding will guard your hearts and your minds in Christ Jesus." Philippians 4:6

How to Help Others

Sometimes you have to be a bit presumptuous when trying to help people in crisis. It may be hard for them to accept others' help, or they may not even realize that things are spiraling out of control. Each of us would probably prefer to be the knight in shining armor than the damsel in distress; unfortunately we don't always have that choice. My advice is to respect someone's privacy, but to not be shy. Your help will be appreciated much more than you (or they) realize. When someone is in the middle of a crisis, it is difficult to keep things in perspective. Your help doesn't need to be anything grandiose. A simple card sent in the mail or even a store-bought treat will mean so very much. It means that you care.

Here are a few ideas of ways to support someone in crisis:

- Listen. Stop and take time to listen to your friend. Don't offer solutions or answers, just listen. They may just need to hear themselves express aloud their thoughts and fears and worries. Respect their confidence, and, as a general rule, do not share with others what you hear. Be patient, be supportive, and just let them unload their burdens onto your shoulders for a little while.

- Household chores. Help with the laundry, cleaning, shopping, or groceries. I kept a list of basic items I needed on my refrigerator (e.g., milk, bananas, bread). Every few days the note would disappear and the groceries or items needed would "magically" appear in our pantry.

- Flowers. If someone will be home to appreciate them, fresh flowers on the kitchen table add life and cheer to what can otherwise be a sad and lonely place.

- Childcare and/or driving. You may not be able to handle this all yourself, but maybe you can coordinate volunteers to help watch children or to drive someone to and from doctor appointments.

- Yard work. A team of young adults can take care of mowing, trimming, and raking leaves in no time. Many Catholic schools and church youth groups are looking for ways to serve others.

- Food. You might not be able to bring a whole meal, but even bread or cookies or packaged foods are welcomed. Coming home to a gift of food on your doorstep is like getting a hug that lasts for hours. If the family is at the hospital, consider bringing them some healthy snacks and waters in a small cooler or disposable container.

- Personal items. This depends on the person and your relationship to them, but some suggestions might include hobby/specialty magazines, bath products, or a manicure coupon. You can help make the hospital room friendlier by bringing photos of the family, small plaques or silk flowers. Our sister-in-law used a color copier to enlarge photos of our boys into simple posters that we hung on Tom's ceiling and wall.

- Financial Support. We were blessed to have good insurance and generous employers, but not everyone is. Offering financial support should be done discretely and with sensitivity. It may be easier for someone to accept money that is designated to cover a specific cost such as school tuition or summer taxes. Gift certificates for restaurants and local stores are also good ideas.

- Religious items. Prayer cards, devotionals, and meditation booklets are easy to read, and often contain writings appropriate to difficult situations. Someone gave us a pamphlet printed by Liguori Publications called "Prayers before Surgery" that we would read through together before Tom's surgeries. Tom also received a religious medal and a relic that he wore on his hospital band. He still wears them both on a simple chain around his neck.

- Cards. So simple and easy to send, and yet so very much appreciated. Whether you have time to write and send a personal note on a weekly basis, or just have time to sign your name to a card, this is a wonderful way to let others know you care and are thinking of them.

- Life's details. When you're in the midst of a crisis, it is easy to forget the little things. My analogy is that it is difficult for a drowning person to call for help when their mouth is full of water. We had family members and friends who stepped in and took care of many details such as canceling upcoming appointments, checking on our insurance coverage, stopping the newspaper, and notifying our Pastor.

"For I was hungry and you gave me something to eat, I was thirsty and you gave me something to drink, I was a stranger and you invited me in, I needed clothes and you clothed me, I was sick and you looked after me, I was in prison and you came to visit me.' Then the righteous will answer him, 'Lord, when did we see you hungry and feed you, or thirsty and give you something to drink? When did we see you a stranger and invite you in, or needing clothes and clothe you? When did we see you sick or in prison and go to visit you?' The King will reply, 'Truly I tell you, whatever you did for one of the least of these brothers and sisters of mine, you did for me.'"
Matthew 25:35-40 (NIV)

Acknowledgements

Although we don't have a record of everyone, below are the names of some of the people who helped us make it through this ordeal . . . We thank you and pray that God may richly bless you!

T.J. and Mary Ackert
Bob and Kim Alexander
Dr. Larry and Susan Allaben
Marie Amante
Ed and Bobby Armbruster
Jim and Linda Badaluco
Mike and Mary Balke
Bill and MaryBeth Barkeley
Bill and Julie Barrett
John and Sue Barthels
Dr. Lee and Karen Begrow
Jack and Mary Bek
David and Joan Bellamy
Frank and Judy Beltman
John and Leslie Berigan
Miguel and Janet Berrios
Scott and Ann Bowen
Lydia Boyce
Steve and Donna Bramble
Fred and Bev Braun
David and Denise Brenner
Mike and Jean Brodie
Ken and Lydia Bruns
Bob and Mary Campbell
Ellen Carpenter
John Carpenter

Rick and Sally Clements
Steve and Mary Cok
Stuart and Nancy Cok
Dave and Chris Coke
Dr. Donald and Sue Condit
George and Sandy Corsiglia
Joe and JoAnn Corsiglia
Tom and Diane Crawford
Mike and MaryAnn Crete
John and Rita Dery
Tom and Ann Dooley
Tim and Lisa Doyle
Fr. Stephen Dudek
Kim and Linda Eadie
Bill and Kathy Ehmann
Bill and Betsi English
Bob and Janet English
Dick and Irene English
Mary Jo English (Benyo)
Tim and Liz English
Tom and Clare English
Dawn Faasse
Fr. Gerry Flater
Barry and Debbie Gair
Sr. Maureen Geary
Casey and Nancy Gillespie

Jeanette Goretzka
Dan and Deb Goris
Tom and Nancy Gutherie
Susan Hagley-Radgens
Joe and Terri Hakeem
Brian Hamel
Steve Haraburda
Dan and Cheryl Heintz
Mark and Val Henderson
John and Mary Hendrickson
Ralph Herpolsheimer
Don and MaryLou Herzog
Rick and Jean Hesse
Dr. Steve and Carol Hickner
Dr. Mike and Sue Jakubowski
Mike and Susan Jandernoa
Mark and Jane Janicki
Dr. Robert Johnson
Sue Kaczkowski
Mark and Katie Kemperman
Dick and Mary Knape
John and Arnette Krauss
Dr. Julian Kuz
Bob and Bernie Lalley
Mike and Kathy Laragy
Janet LeMier (Veldhouse)
Jim and Betty LeRoy
Tom and Carol Lindsey
Jay and Colleen Lowe
Chris and Barb Madura
Charlie and Ann Malaney
Jeff and Janice Martin
Becky McCormack

Dr. David and Julie McCorry
Bill and Donna McDonagh
Pat and Julie Mead
Joe and Karen Melton
Sr. Ann Michael
Jennifer Milas
Mitch and Ginger Mileski
David and Lil Mohan
Marcia Moncion
Lyle Morrison
Bill and Mary Morrissey
John and Lou Morrow
Mark and Kathy Morrow
Pat and Lisa Morrow
Tom and Laura Murphy
Sandy Nelson
Tim and Kathleen Nickerson
Larry and Kathy Nienhaus
Bill and Marty Norman
Mark and Maureen Norton
Dan and Karen O'Rourke
Brian and Betsy Pangle
Ron and Alicia Parinin
Pat and Vicki Patton
Brian and Denise Plachta
George and Dolores Powell
Dr. Ernie and Mary Quiroz
Mike and Deanna Reams
Mel Reed
Fr. Julian Reginato
Ben and Barb Rietema
Mark and Diane Rizik
Greg and MaryJane Robinson

Dr. Carlos Rodriguez
Jerry and Patty Rohen
Bob and Phyllis Rosenbach
Tom and Tracy Rosenbach
Linda Schetz
Jack and MaryCay Schmieder
Matt and Annie Schmieder
Jim and MaryKay Schumar
Dr. Bruce and Joy
   Schuurmann
Dave and Cheri Seamon
Tom and Janet Sennett
Tom and Susan Shearer
Debbie Shearer-Rosenfeld
Merle and Barb Shoemaker
Wayne and Lyndy Simon
Dr. Marc and Barbi Sink
Gary Smith
Kevin and Mary Smith
Terri Smith
Mike and Kathy Smolenski
Tom and Pat Sommerdyk
Elaine Sowa
Dr. William Stawski
Chuck and Bobbi Stevens
Fr. Len Sudlik
Patti Swets
Steve and Jean Talaga
Lou and Julie Tessier
Deb Tiejema

Joe and Ruth Tierney
Paul and Mary Timmons
Gary and Jeannine Toth
Dr. Steven Triesenberg
Gary Vachon
Ruth Vachon
Dr. Jim and Cheryl
   VanDaalen
Jay VanDaalen
Jean VanDaalen
Dr. Christopher VandenBerg
Jack and Amy VanOverloop
Fr. Steve Vasek
Kenn and Barb Vidro
Fr. Peter Vu
Paul Wang
Karen Weber
Scott Weber
Ron and Shelley Webster
Dr. Phil and Cathy Weighner
Dr. Rick Wilcox
Linda and Frank Willetts
Steve and Kim Willison
Barth and Theresa Wilson
Dr. Jeffery Wilt
Paul Winn
Jim and Carol Yost
Dr. Tony Youn
Ann Zoellner
Tom and Dorothy Zoellner

Teachers and students at IHM School
ICU Nurses (especially Pam, Sharon, Linda, Cathy, Janet, and Elizabeth)
Respiratory Therapists (especially Kathy L. and Tim)
Aquinas College
Superior Business Solutions
Occupational Therapists (especially Dave, Norma, and Meghan)
Physical Therapists (especially John D., Tim, and Beth)
Burn Unit staff (especially Dr. Wilcox, Bonnie, Stephan, Debbie, Marti, Sheri, Kate, and Dave)
Mary Free Bed Rehabilitation Hospital

. . . . and many, many other friends, relatives, and strangers who sent cards and (more importantly) who held us up in prayer throughout this ordeal. Thank you—your actions and petitions made all the difference!